# Use Libr Writer

THOMAS ECCLESTONE

# DEDICATION

To Julian Robinson, without whose help I'd never have been able to
complete this book.

# CONTENTS

# 1 FIRST STEPS

❶ Go to http://www.LibreOffice.org/download/LibreOffice-fresh/ in your browser

❷ Click on the version of LibreOffice that you want to download. The screenshots in this guide are taken from version 4.2.5 for windows.

**DOWNLOAD VERSION 4.2.5**

❸ If using chrome, the following box will appear at the bottom of the screen while the download is taking place. An estimate of how long the download will take is also shown.

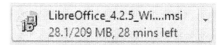

❹ Once the download is finished, the following will appear at the bottom of the screen in chrome.

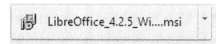

Other web browsers will vary.

Congratulations, you're ready to run the installer!

## Step Two - Install

**1** Click on the LibreOffice install program. You can either find it at the bottom of your screen in chrome:

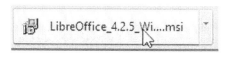

Or by opening File Explorer  and selecting the download folder:

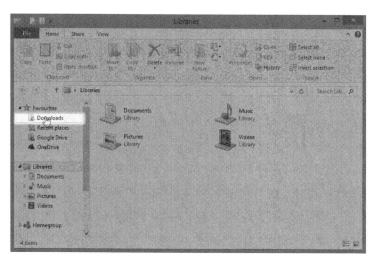

Then double clicking on the installer

❷ The LibreOffice installation wizard will appear

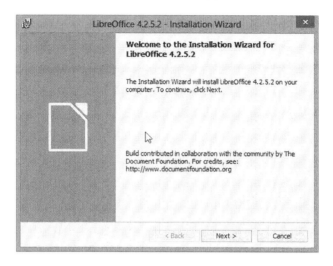

Click on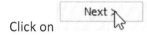

❸ In the next dialogue you will be given the option of a typical or custom install. I recommend simply using the typical install.

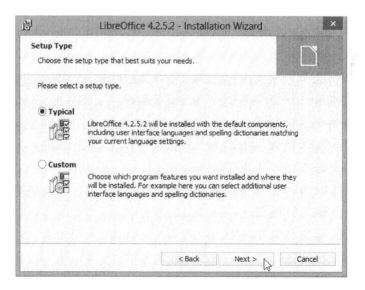

If you are happy with the typical install click

If you want to install a custom installation see "How to run a custom installation" below.

**4** The next screen gives you a few more options. I recommend you click on install

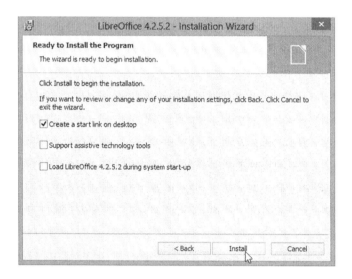

Selecting ☑ Support assistive technology tools will install tools that LibreOffice provides for people with various disabilities.

Selecting ☑ Load LibreOffice 4.2.5.2 during system start-up will mean that LibreOffice will start when the operating system starts. It's useful if you use LibreOffice almost all the time but may slow down loading the operating system.

When you are happy with your options click Install . If you are not happy with any choice you've made you can go back to an earlier choice by clicking < Back .

**5** A user account dialogue will appear. Click "Yes", "Allow" or "Ok".

❻A progress dialogue will appear:

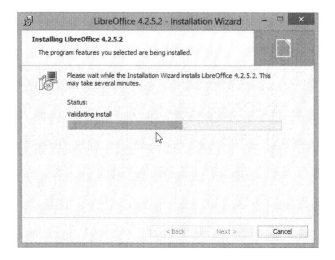

Wait until it is finished

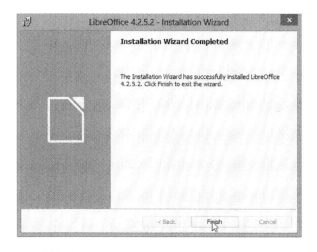

and click on Finish .

## How to run a custom installation

 Run the install procedure above, but in step  instead of selecting

**● Typical**

LibreOffice 4.2.5.2 will be installed with the default components, including user interface languages and spelling dictionaries matching your current language settings.

select

**● Custom**

Choose which program features you want installed and where they will be installed. For example here you can select additional user interface languages and spelling dictionaries.

Then click on

 To find out if there is available space for the feature set you've

selected click on

The following dialogue will appear:

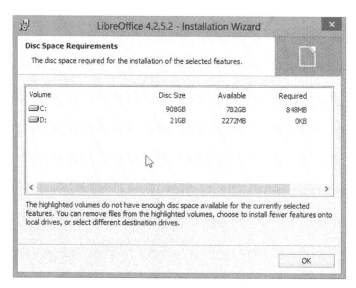

Notice that the column Available shows how much space your disk contains, and Required shows how much disk space your installation has available.

In the above example, we're good to go.

Click 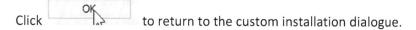 to return to the custom installation dialogue.

③ To change the location the program will install to select change

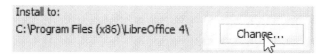

A location selection dialogue will appear:

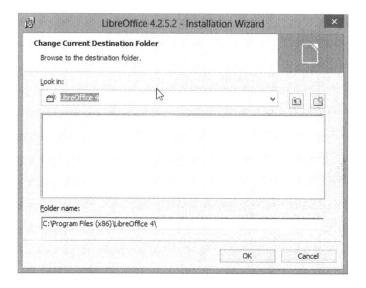

Clicking on the ⌄ next to the look in location will provide you with a list of folders

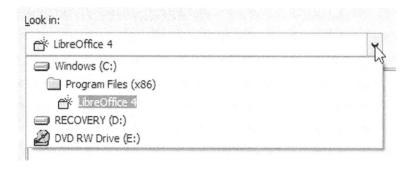

which you can select from, going up or down as necessary.

You can add a new folder by selecting

Or you can simply type the file location in the box provided

I don't recommend changing the file location UNLESS your default drive doesn't have enough room for the installation to work.

❸ To install a new language

Click on the next to [+] Additional user interface languages

A list of languages will appear:

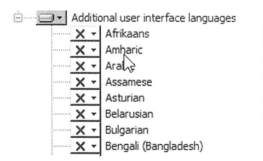

Scroll down to the language you want, and click on the X ▾

Select ![This feature will be installed on local hard drive.] if you want it installed on the local hard drive or

![This feature, and all sub-features, will be installed on local hard drive.] if you want sub features such as spell check and custom fonts to be installed. I recommend this option.

**4** To install non-English language dictionaries:

Click on the ⊞ next to ⊞ ▭▾ Optional Components

Click on the ⊞ next to ⊞ ▭▾ Dictionaries

Scroll down to the dictionary you want, and click on the X ▾ by its name, for example:

X ▾ Bengali

Select

![This feature, and all sub-features, will be installed on local hard drive.]

**5** Other Optional Components

LibreOffice installs most components by default. The only exception is ActiveX components. If you don't need a particular component and you are low on space you can click the ▭▾ by its name and select

![X This feature will not be available.] but I do not recommend doing this. It will limit the facilities your LibreOffice installation can provide to you.

Some people may need ActiveX controls, in which case you can select the X ▾ by X ▾ ActiveX Control and

![This feature, and all sub-features, will be installed on local hard drive.] . I don't recommend doing this unless you know that you will need ActiveX controls since it can slow down LibreOffice and it's an unusual requirement

**6** Once happy with the options you have selected click on

 . A File type dialogue will appear

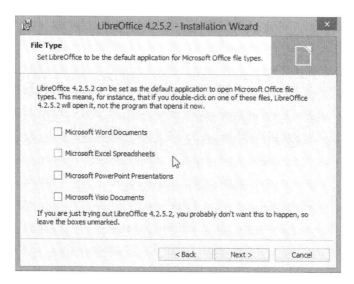

I recommend leaving the defaults on this, but simply check the box next to the file types you want to associate LibreOffice with and click

 when you are happy.

**7** You are now on the installation dialogue that is the last step in "Install LibreOffice" above.

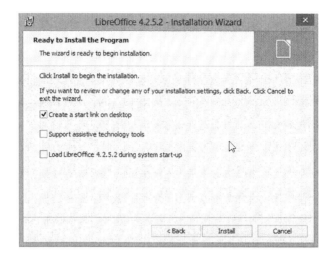

Selecting ☑ Support assistive technology tools will install tools that LibreOffice provides for people with various disabilities.

Selecting ☑ Load LibreOffice 4.2.5.2 during system start-up will mean that LibreOffice will start when the operating system starts. It's useful if you use LibreOffice almost all the time but may slow down loading the operating system.

When you are happy with your options click Install . If you are not happy with any choice you've made you can go back to an earlier choice by clicking < Back .

❽ A user account control dialogue may appear. Click "Ok", "Yes" or "Allow" depending on what version of windows you use.

❾ A progress dialogue will appear.

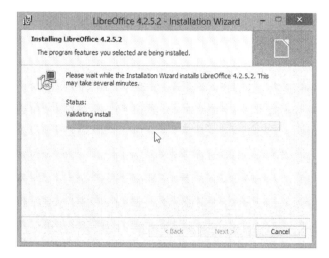

Wait until the installer finishes:

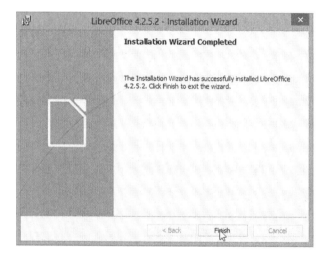

And click on  .

## To Run

To run LibreOffice Text writer double click on its icon on the desktop or select its tile in the start screen  or search for it:

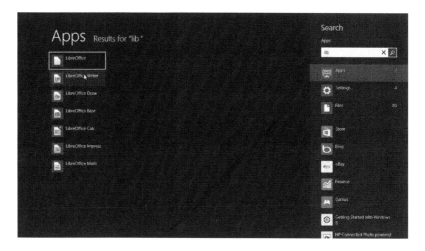

## Create a New Document

If you've started the main LibreOffice program you will see the following window:

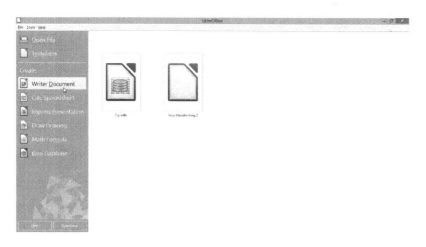

To create a new document click on:

## To open an existing document

In the main LibreOffice window, click on

Select the file you want to open:

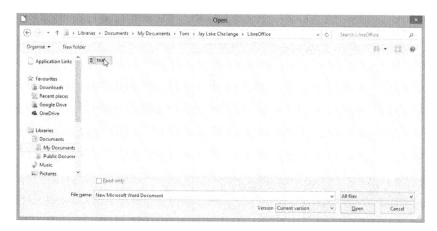

✓And click .

You will see the LibreOffice Writer screen for the first time:

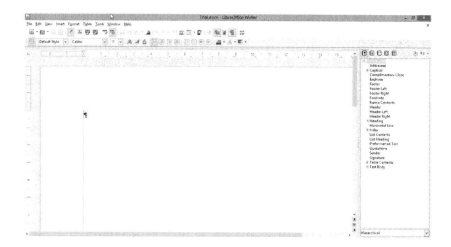

In the next chapter, we'll use LibreOffice Writer to write a simple letter, spell check it, and print it out!

# 2 WRITE A LETTER

This chapter is intended to give you the basic information you need to write a letter or other simple document in LibreOffice. It will show you:

1. How to write text in LibreOffice
2. How to do some basic formatting
3. A tab stop, so you can line up the address on the right hand corner
4. Basic formatting - how to change the font, font size, add emphasis.
5. How to save the document
6. How to print the document

That's a lot of material to cover in one chapter! But by the end of this chapter you should know almost everything that you need to write the basic documents that you use every day!

## Getting to know LibreOffice Writer.

When you open LibreOffice Writer on a new document you will see a screen that looks like the following:

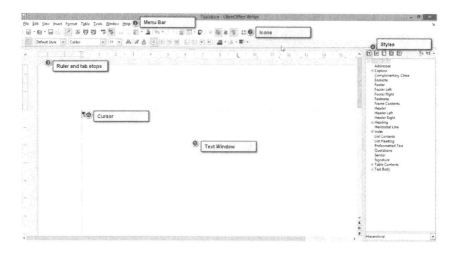

It is comprised of a number of features that allow you to control the program:

①Menu Bar

The menu bar provides a simple way to control the program. Each menu has a specific purpose that allows you to remember what options are available.

**File** This contains things like opening, saving, printing and closing files. It also contains standard wizards that allow you to quickly make specific types of files such as letters etc.

**Edit** Allows you to undo, redo, copy and paste, track changes, and many other editing features

**View** Controls what LibreOffice displays including toolbars, icons, and zoom.

**Insert** This allows you to add things like hyperlinks, charts, images, and many other advanced features.

**Format** Allows you to control the appearance of text, add special characters like the copyright symbol and the layout of the page.

**Table** This menu item allows you to insert, control, and change tables (for example tables of figures, tables of content, they are also used to control the layout of items on pages sometimes).

**Tools** Include spelling, word count, mail merge and many other facilities.

**Window** Open a new window so you can work on more than one place in the document at a time.

**Help** An important menu - used to get help about the program, find out information about LibreOffice itself, and send feedback to the development team.

Obviously the above might seem confusing at first but as you follow through this beginners guide you will soon get the hang of things. At first you only need a small subset of the features before you start to produce documents in the program.

## ②Icons
These icons provide a quick way to access features that are commonly used in LibreOffice. Where an icon is provided it allows you to select that specific feature without going through the menu system.

## ③Ruler and Tab Stops
When laying out text you can use the ruler as a quick way of seeing where text will appear on the page.

Tab stops are used so that all the text that follows the tab stop is placed on the same location on the screen.

## ④Styles
LibreOffice is considered a style manager. A style is something like a chapter header, emphasis, or title which always contains the same format. This allows you to have a uniform look to the document.

## ⑤Text Window / Area
The text window is where you will spend the majority of your time in LibreOffice. The document text that you are writing will be displayed

here.

### ⑥ Cursor

The cursor is a (normally flashing) line. It shows you where the text you are about to type will appear.

Now you know something about the first screen in LibreOffice Text writer you're ready to actually write a letter!

## Writing Some Text

Hover the mouse over the text window so that it's cursor changes to ⌶ . Click once.

Start to type:

This·is·the·first·thing·that·I·have·typed·in·LibreOffice¶

What you are typing should appear on the screen.

Press backspace until you've deleted everything, then type out the first line of a letter:

29·Fictitious·street,¶

Press enter / return to go to the next line, and keep on typing until you've written a letter.

29·Fictitious·street,¶

Unknown·Town¶

County,¶

PostCode,¶

20/7/2014,¶

Dear·Gran,¶

I've·just·started·to·use·LibreOffice·Text·writer·and·it's·great!¶

Love,¶

Thomas·Ecclestone.¶

## Putting the Address over to the right hand side of the document

You've typed out a letter - and it was easy! Well done!

But there's a problem with it. The formatting just isn't right. The convention is to put the address onto the right hand side of the screen.

This is where **Tab Stops** come in useful.

### ①Select the address and date

Move the mouse to the end of the text you want to select. In this case, the comma after the date. Click the left mouse button and hold it down. Then move the mouse to the beginning of the section you want to highlight. In this case, the beginning of the first line of the address.

Let the mouse button go.

You should see the text highlighted.

29·Fictitious·street,¶

Unknown·Town¶

County,¶

PostCode,¶

20/7/2014,¶

Dear·Gran,¶

I've·just·started·to·use·LibreOffice·Text·writer·and·it's·great!¶

Love,¶

Thomas·Ecclestone.¶

If you don't, then click anywhere on the screen and try it again until you've got it right.

② Move the tab stop
Look at the Ruler at the top of the screen

There is an upside down triangle ▽ hover the mouse over it and it will go black ▼. Click and hold the mouse down and drag it to the right. Let go when you get to the number 6.

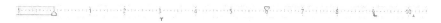

Notice the upside down triangle is remains on 6, and the letter text has moved.

29·Fictitious·street,¶

Unknown·Town¶

County,¶

PostCode,¶

20/7/2014,¶

Dear·Gran,¶

I've·just·started·to·use·LibreOffice·Text·writer·and·it's·great!¶

Move the mouse down to the end of the word Gran and click once.
Notice that the tab stop returns to the original position.

29·Fictitious·street,¶

Unknown·Town¶

County,¶

PostCode,¶

20/7/2014,¶

Dear·Gran,¶

### How to Change the Font

Your grandmother will love receiving your letter- but she'd prefer to be
able to read it! Maybe it would be nice to increase the size of font? And
while you're at it, it might be nice to change it so it looks more like a
handwritten letter.

①Highlight the entire document

On the right hand side of the text window is a scroll bar.

Left click and hold down and the scroll bar will go black:

When you move the mouse up or down the document will go up or down. Move the scroll bar down until you can see the end of the document you've written.

②Highlight the entire document

Left click at the end of the document, hold the mouse button down, then move the mouse upwards and to the left until you've highlighted the entire document.

Let go of the mouse button.

③ Change the Font

Click on the font button (label 1) and type in Script. Press enter.

Notice that the font that you are using has changed.

Click on the font size box (label 2 above) and type 16 then press enter.

You can see that the font size had changed.

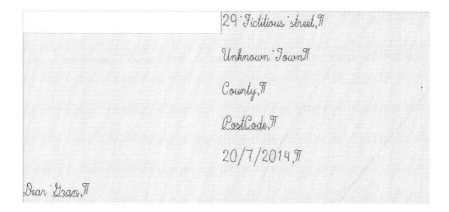

29 Fictitious street,¶

Unknown Town¶

County,¶

PostCode,¶

20/7/2014,¶

Dear Gran,¶

Hover the mouse cursor over the word great, and double click (rapidly click the left mouse button twice making sure not to wait for too long between clicks). The word Great will be highlighted.

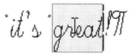

it's great!¶

Move the mouse to the icons at the top of the screen

Left click on the big A (label 1).

Notice that the word Great has been given some emphasis.

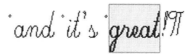

and it's great!¶

Congratulations, you've changed the font, the font size, and learned how to bold or give a word some emphasis.

④ Save the document with a new file name

It's all very well to write a letter but sometimes you might want to save it as well so you can work on it later, or in case the post doesn't turn up and you want to print it out again.

Fortunately, that's a pretty easy process in LibreOffice.

First, hover the mouse over the File menu, then click on Save As which (label 1 on the diagram).

A save as dialogue will be displayed.

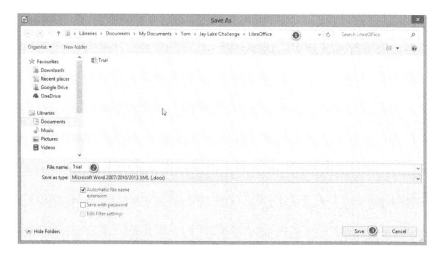

You can use it like any other "Save As" dialogue. Change the directory you are going to save in using the directory box (label 1), the name using the File Name field (label 2) and then press save (label 3) to save the file to disk.

If you get a dialogue that says that the file contains formatting that can't be saved using the current file type select ODT format. I'll go into more detail about saving documents in different formats at a later point in the book.

⑤Print the Letter

**Note: To print a document you need to have a working printer attached to your computer. Only follow these instructions if this is the case.**

First, in the File menu select Page Preview (1)

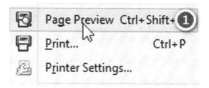

This will make LibreOffice display a window that shows you what the document you are about to print out looks like. While you can print a document without doing a Page Preview there is a chance that you will end up printing something that you don't want to or seeing a mistake that you've made after you've wasted paper.

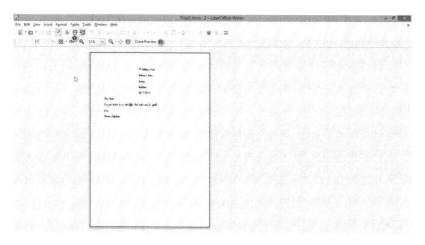

If you are not happy with the document that you're printing press

Close Preview

(2) otherwise if you want to print the entire document to the default printer press Print File Directly (1).

In a later chapter I'll describe how to print particular pages or to specific printers.

### Next Chapter

In this chapter we've described some of the main features of LibreOffice. You should be able to use LibreOffice to do some basic formatting, print out a document, and save a document. You should know the main features of LibreOffice Writer.

In the next chapter I'm going to go further: showing you how to use formatting to make a document look nice and how to spell check your document.

# 3 HOW TO FORMAT A DOCUMENT

In this chapter we will go into far more detail about how to change fonts, line spacing, and other features that allow you to control the appearance of text in a document. LibreOffice Writer is a fully powered Style Editor which allows you to have a huge amount of control in how your document is typeset.

## Highlighting Text.

When formatting existing text you need to select it first. You can do this by going to the end of the text that you want to format, pressing the left mouse button down, then moving the mouse up and to the left until you've highlighted the entire section.

It's easy to see the area you've highlighted because the background of the text changes to light blue:

This·is ·some·highlighted·text

## Basic Formatting: Bold

First, highlight the text you want to bold

This·is ·some·highlighted·text

In the Taskbar click on the bold icon 🅐 or press control and b at the same time.

## This·is·some·highlighted·text⁴

The font changes to bold. If you click on the bold icon 🅐 or press control and b a second time you will toggle bold off again:

## This·is·some·highlighted·text⁴

### Other Basic Formatting

In the same way by highlighting some text and then clicking on the following icons you can make the text italic or underlined.

| Type | Icon | Shortcut | Example |
|------|------|----------|---------|
| Italic | | Control + i | |
| Underline | | Control + U | |

### Changing Text Colour

Sometimes you might want to change the colour of the documents text.

First, highlight the text. Then, look for the font colour icon 🅰 ˅ note that under the 'A' is a block of colour. If you click on the 'A' the text will change to that colour (which is the default text colour).

Alternatively, click on the down arrow ˅ to the right of 🅰 . A colour selection dialogue will appear. Click on the colour that you want.

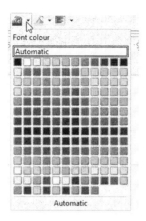

You should see the text change colour:

This·is·some·highlighted·text

However, once you click off the text you may find that any further text you type will be the colour you've just chosen. If you want to type in the default colour click on the down arrow again and click on automatic:

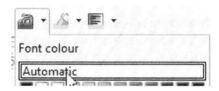

This will restore you to the default text colour. If you've got a section of text where you've changed the background to another colour you can return it to the default by highlighting it and then selecting automatic as well.

### Highlighting some text

When you have something that is particularly important you may want to highlight it.

First, select the text that you want to highlight:

# This·is·some·highlighted·text¶

The highlight icon looks like ![icon] ▾ . Again, under ![icon] is a block of colour which is the colour that LibreOffice would use to highlight the selection if you simply click on the icon:

# This·is·some·highlighted·text◀

Don't worry that the text appears a slightly different colour to the one you've selected. This is because the text is highlighted. When you click off, you see the actual document colour

# This·is·some·highlighted·text◀

Again, you don't have to just use the default highlight colour. By pressing the down arrow ▾ you can select from a larger range of colours, or return the selection to the default background colour using

> No Fill

.

## Background Colour

Background colour is not like highlight colour because it is the default colour for one or more lines of text. While you can still use highlight on specific words in the line if you select "No Fill" when you've selected a background colour your document will return to the background colour you've selected rather than white.

Select the line(s) you want to change:

> This·is·some·highlighted·text¶
> Another·line¶
> and·another¶
> ¶

Hit the ⊟ if you're happy with the current selection of background colour (remember, it's the block of colour under ⊟ ) or the down arrow ˅ if like me you want to select another background colour.

If you want to return to the normal default background colour click on the down arrow and select No Fill which returns you to the default setting.

### Non-Printing Characters.

You might have noticed so far that when you're typing sometimes LibreOffice shows you some strange symbols which it doesn't print.

For example, at the end of every line you type you see the following symbol ¶ or every time you press the space bar LibreOffice Writer displays ˙ .

These are called non-printing characters. Many people like to see these symbols because they can help prevent you making mistakes such as having two spaces in a row where you only intend one. Other people don't like them.

If they are on, look at the taskbar and you should see a symbol that looks like: ¶ click on the icon, and it will turn to ¶ . Look at the text and the non-printing characters have disappeared!

# This is some highlighted text
# Another line
# and another

## Text Alignment

When writing a document you sometimes find that you may want to change whether words appear on the left (as normal) or the right, or centred, or justified:

This text is left aligned

This text is centred

This text is right aligned

This text is justified. This text is justified. This text is justified. This text is justified. This text is justified as is this.

Left, centred, or right aligned is obvious. But what does justified do? Where a document is left aligned each space is the same width. This means that there is a ragged edge to each line. Where you justify text LibreOffice automatically changes the width of spaces so each line ends in the same place.

To set the text alignment first select the text that you want to align then click the appropriate icon or use the shortcut from the table below:

| Alignment | Icon | Shortcut |
|---|---|---|
| Left Align | | Ctrl+L |
| Centre Align | | Ctrl+E |
| Right Align | | Ctrl+R |
| Justify | | Ctrl+J |

**Bullet point lists**

A bullet point list is often used:

- When you are summarising points
- When you are giving short factual information or,
- in examples in user guides!

It's pretty easy to make a bullet point list in LibreOffice Writer.

Press ⊞ in the taskbar.

Type the first item in the list, then press enter

- This is the first item in the list
- |

repeat the process until you've populated the list completely

- This is the first item in the list
- This is the second
- This is the third
- 

Once you've finished populating the list, press enter again.

There's one thing that can confuse some people. If you have a bullet point list and you want to add an explanation of your point on the next line you can end up with something that looks like this:

- This is the first item in the list
- An explanation of the item
- This is the second
- This is the third
- |

which isn't what you want. Select the text that you don't want to include in the list, and then press the bullet point list icon [icon] .

- This is the first item in the list
An explanation of the item
- This is the second
- This is the third
- 

but it still doesn't look right, does it? You want to indent it to the same level as the bullet point list. It's easy to do that. Just press the increase indent icon [icon] until you are happy with the result.

- This is the first item in the list
     An explanation of the item
- This is the second
- This is the third
- 

## Basic numbered lists

Where you might want to refer to an item in a list it is often useful to give each item a number. You can make a numbered list in the same way as you made a bullet point list. The only difference is that you should use the numbering icon [icon] instead of the bullet point list icon.

## More Advanced List Formatting

Sometimes the basic bullet point list formatting just doesn't seem that adventurous. LibreOffice Writer gives you the option to control the appearance of lists.

First, select the text that you want to highlight.

Then, in the Format menu, click on Bullets and numbering

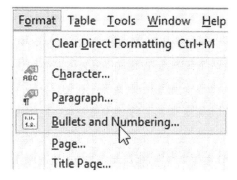

A bullets and numbering dialogue will be displayed.

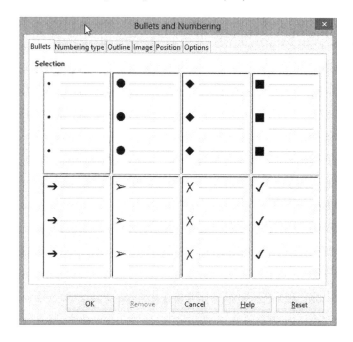

Select the bullet point that you want, or if you want a numbered list click on Numbering type. There are several other list types that you can use as well... experiment and see what different options look like!

One of the options that might be very useful are the Outline options since this means that list items on different levels of indentation are numbered as if they are sub points:

1. First line
   (a) Second Line
2. Third Line

which is often used in legal documents.

## Increasing and Decreasing the Indent

If you want to increase or decrease the indentation of a line of text, put the cursor anywhere in the line of text and press the increase indent icon or the decrease indent icon .

To increase or decrease the indentation of a block of lines of text highlight it and then press the increase indent icon or the decrease indent icon .

This is how you
increase the indent
of several lines of text
at a go.

## Next Chapter

This chapter has discussed some basic methods of formatting documents. Later on in the book I'm going to discuss many other formatting methods, but before I do I want to show you some of the very useful tools that LibreOffice offers writers.

It's nice to make a document look good but it's even better if the spelling is right!

# 4 MAKING CORRECTIONS, TOOLS, AND OTHER COOL FEATURES.

LibreOffice provides a lot of bang for your buck. In this chapter I'm going to show you some of the tools that make it easy to automate tasks that would otherwise take quite some time and effort. In particular I'm going to cover the following tasks:

- How to undo changes, and redo changes
- How to use tools including spell checker and word count
- How to create headers and footers
- How to export files to other formats.

## How to use Undo and Redo

Everyone makes mistakes. LibreOffice, like most modern programs, provides a simple multi-level undo feature that allows you to correct them without any real problems.

Say you have the following document:

This is a document that I am writing.
LibreOffice is great, and it's nice to be able to make a mistake and fix it.

By accident you delete part of the text

This is a document it's nice to be able to make a mistake and fix it.

All you need to do is click on  and the document will return to normal.

However, if you've made multiple changes pressing the ⌄ to the right of the undo icon will produce a list of all the changes that you have made.

To undo all the steps up to a specific point in time simply click on that step.

If you undo too many steps LibreOffice allows you to press ⤻ to go forward one step at a time, or you can press ˇ to get a list of the steps you've undeleted. Clicking on one will redo all the steps up to that point.

## Using automatic spell checking

By default LibreOffice Writer automatically spell checks as you type. When you press certain buttons such as full stop or enter LibreOffice checks the sentence for errors and underlines any potential errors in red.

This docckument hass a lot of errorss

Right clicking on a word with an error produces a list of suggestions.

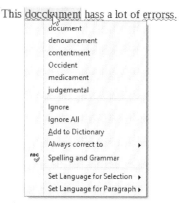

Clicking on one of the suggestions will change the word to that suggestion.

## Ignore a word or Ignore all instances of a word using the automatic spell check

Sometimes you don't want LibreOffice to correct a word but you don't want to add it to the dictionary which applies to all documents. For example if you are writing a science fiction novel using unusual terms which would be incorrect in other contexts.

LibreOffice allows you to ignore a specific error instance by right clicking on the word and then clicking on ignore

Ignore . Alternatively, you might want to ignore all instances of that word in the document, in which case you can select Ignore All .

Before using the Ignore or Ignore All feature you should make sure that the word is spelled correctly. LibreOffice won't alert you to the word again (if you select Ignore) or any other instance of the word (ignore all) so if it's wrong it is unlikely that you will pick up the mistake.

### Adding a word to the dictionary using automatic spell check

**Warning: it is very important to make sure that any word you add to the dictionary is spelled correctly.**

To add a word to the dictionary right click on the word and select "Add to dictionary" Add to Dictionary . LibreOffice will take this word to be a valid English language word (even if the word is in fact incorrect).

### Always correct with automatic spell check

This is another dangerous feature although it can be useful. Say, you always accidentally write that when you mean that. Right clicking on that and then hovering over Always correct to ▸ will produce a list of corrections. Simply choose the one that you want. From that point LibreOffice will automatically correct the word.

## Changing language for a word or paragraph

It's often the case that you might want to use a foreign word or quotation. While LibreOffice has a language set for the entire document it's also possible to set a language option for a word or paragraph.

For example, the following is a quotation written in French:

*Il n'y a qu' un bonheur dans la vie, c'est d'aimer et d'être aimé.*

To specify that the word 'bonheur' is French, right click on it, then hover the mouse over   Set Language for Selection ▶   and select the language you want to use.

Alternatively select   None (Do not check spelling)   if LibreOffice doesn't have a dictionary for the language.

If you change your mind you can also reset the selection to the default language by clicking on Reset to Default Language .

Note that with the above options you can change the language for more than a word by highlighting a section of text. Alternatively, if you want to change the language for the entire paragraph right click on a spelling mistake, then hover the mouse over Set Language for Paragraph ▶ .

### Turning off (or on) the automatic spell check
While many people like automatic spell checking other people find the existence of red underlining as they're writing very distracting. If you

want to turn off the automatic spell check simply click on the icon

. You can always turn it on again by clicking on ABC again.

### How to use the Spell Check and Grammar check
While the automatic spell check is very useful many people will want to run a full spelling or grammar check because it has additional facilities.

To start the spell check press function key 7(F7) or click on spelling and grammar on the tools menu.

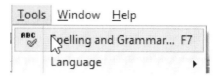

LibreOffice will display a Spelling and Grammar dialogue, see below:

## Text Language

The first thing you see in the Spelling and Grammar dialogue is the text language that LibreOffice is checking against.

If you click on the down arrow ⌄ it will provide you with a list of other languages. If the language you're writing isn't English, simply select the correct language from the list.

## Ignore / Ignore All

Notice that the next thing you see is an error dialogue with suggestions beneath it. In this case, LibreOffice doesn't recognise the French word Il. It's suggesting the English word I.

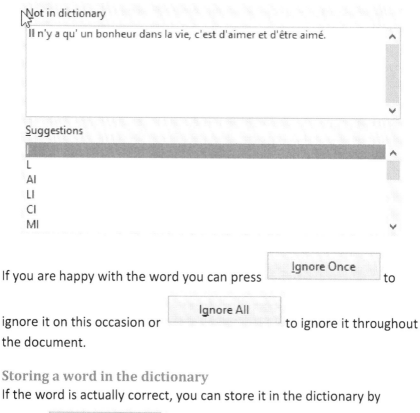

If you are happy with the word you can press [ Ignore Once ] to ignore it on this occasion or [ Ignore All ] to ignore it throughout the document.

## Storing a word in the dictionary

If the word is actually correct, you can store it in the dictionary by clicking [ Add to Dictionary ]. In future LibreOffice will treat this word as an English language word. It may even suggest it.

## Making corrections

If you double click on one of the suggestions LibreOffice will replace the unknown word with the suggestion once. Alternatively, you can single

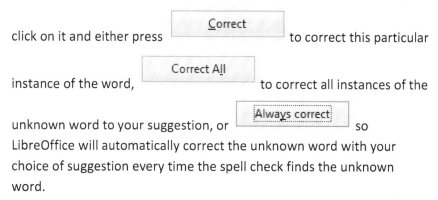

click on it and either press [ Correct ] to correct this particular instance of the word, [ Correct All ] to correct all instances of the unknown word to your suggestion, or [ Always correct ] so LibreOffice will automatically correct the unknown word with your choice of suggestion every time the spell check finds the unknown word.

## Undo a change

Sometimes, everyone makes a mistake. If you accept a correction when you shouldn't have, simply press [ Undo ] and LibreOffice will undo the correction.

## Close the spell check

If you decide you want to stop spell checking press [ Close ].

## Finding out the word count of a document

If you're producing a assignment or article you sometimes want to know how many words you've written in a particular selection or the whole document. If you want to find out the number of words in a section of the document select the text and then click on Word Count in the Tools menu. LibreOffice will count the words in the entire document whether you've selected some text or not.

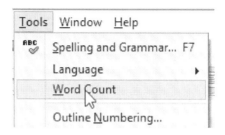

Once you've clicked on Word Count, LibreOffice will produce the word count dialogue:

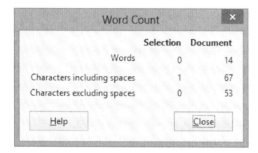

One important thing to note is that different word processors calculate number of words in slightly different ways so there might be a slight discrepancy between the figures that LibreOffice produces and the figures that Microsoft word produces. This is ordinary and nothing to be worried about.

Click  to close the dialogue.

### How To Make Headers
Click on the portion of the document above the dotted line (i.e. the area that is part of the top border)

On the left hand side you'll see the following:

Click on the + sign. LibreOffice Writer will create a header.

Then click into the header. You can do this by clicking at the top left hand corner of the screen.

Start typing.

You've added a basic header, so congratulations. You can close the header by clicking on any line of text in the document.

## Including Page Number, Count, or other Special Fields in the Header

Sometimes you might want to include page numbers, dates, page counts or other automatically generated information in a header. While you are in the header go to Fields in the Insert menu.

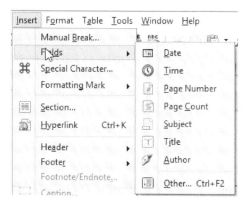

Select Date, Time, Page Number etc as appropriate. Note that in the header the field will be highlighted.

Although the highlight won't show when you print the document. It's just there to show that it is automatically generated by LibreOffice.

## Different Headers on First Page, Odd and Even pages.

Often when someone makes a more complicated document, they might want to suppress headers on the first page, or have different headers on odd and even pages.

On the dotted line under the header there is

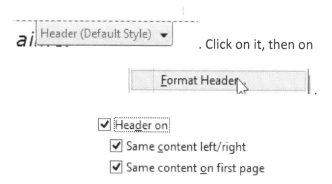

. Click on it, then on

Uncheck the box for same content left/right if you want different content on odd and even pages, or same content on first page if you want a different header on the first page of the document.

**Note** that when you select these options you will have to make a header on each type of page. So, you'll have to make a header on an odd and an even page if you uncheck same content left/right. And you'll have to make a header on the first page as well as the second if you uncheck Same content on first page.

### Delete a header
On the dotted line under the header there is

 . Click on it, then on

Delete Header... . You'll have to click on to confirm that you want to delete it. You can't change your mind if you delete a header.

## Borders and Shading.
Sometimes you might want to visually show that text is in a header or footer. If you want to do this,

click on  then on

Border and Background...

You get the Border / background dialogue.

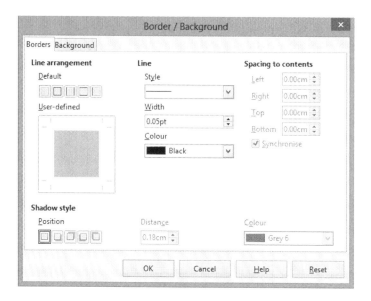

You can select a user defined outline or shadow style in the above dialogue.

Most of the options work as you would expect, but notice that the user-defined option allows you to specify particular lines by clicking at the top, bottom, left or right of the square.

You can specify line type and width using the Line options.

**Line**

Style

Width

0.05pt

Colour

Black

And you can also add drop shadows to the header using the Shadow Style options.

**Shadow style**

Position

Sometimes you may want to change the colour of the header. Click on the Background tab to see a colour selection dialogue. Select the colour you want.

Notice that you can't undo changes using the normal undo feature in this dialogue; you can reset the header to the original settings, and you can cancel your changes.

### Making a Footer
The same features are all available for footers. To make a footer instead of a header all you do is click in the text window at the bottom of the document.

### Export File to Other Formats
While LibreOffice has its own .ODT format, sometimes you may want to

send a file to someone who uses Microsoft Word, or send a file in .pdf format.

It's simple to save a document in another format.

In the File menu, click on Save As Save As... Ctrl+Shift+S .

LibreOffice will show a Save As dialogue

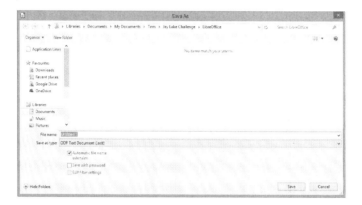

Make sure your file name and directory is correct, then look beneath the File Name box. You'll see an option that says Save as Type

in this case you're saving the document as an ODF Text Document. Click on the down arrow ⌄ and LibreOffice will show a list of file types.

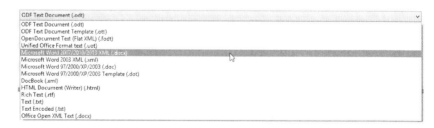

Click on the file type that you want.

Then save the file by clicking  .

## Opening a File using a non-ODF format

But wait! It's all very well being able to export a file in different formats. But it's even nicer to be able to open and edit it. LibreOffice makes that easy.

In the File menu select open 📭 Open...                    Ctrl+O . An open dialogue will be shown.

Make sure you are in the correct directory first.

If you look at the dialogue you'll notice that at the right of the File Name field there is a box that contains the name of a file type (in this case ODF Text Document). Click on ODF Text Document (*.odt) ⌄ . Note that the box could say another file type such as

Office Open XML Text Templat ⌄ or any number of other types.

LibreOffice will show a list of file types:

You can scroll up or down to show more format types. Click on the file type you want to open. I'd suggest .docx (Microsoft Word) format:

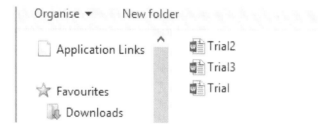

The files dialogue will display all files of that type in your current directory.

Double click on the file you want to open.

## Next Chapter

We've covered a lot in this chapter. I've shown you how to export files to formats supported by other word processors, how to check spelling, as well as headers and footers. These tools are things you will use on a regular basis.

In the next chapter I'm going to introduce you to some basic techniques for improving the presentation of documents.

I think you'll enjoy it.

# 5 IMAGES

So far we've show you how to produce documents that are entirely text based. And in the 1980's that would probably have been a vast improvement on typewriter technology. But admit it - you're hankering for pretty pictures and more creative desktop design.

And what's wrong with that.

### How to Insert an Image
Say you've got a simple plain text document that you want to make more interesting

This is a boring text document.
Nothing to see here.

First, put the cursor to the position you want to insert the image. In the Insert menu hover the mouse over Image, and then select "From File."

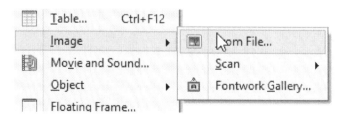

An Insert Image dialogue will appear. Change the directory to the correct one, then double click on the image file you want to insert.

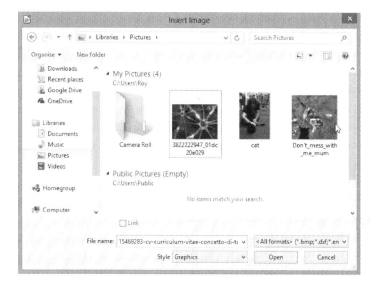

LibreOffice will insert the image into your file. You often find that the image is too large or small, or not in the correct place.

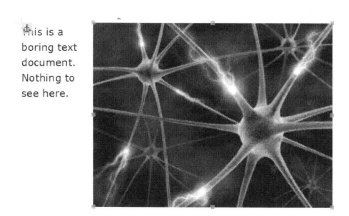

This is a boring text document. Nothing to see here.

### How to Move an Image.

Moving an image is easy. Put the mouse pointer over the image, then click and hold the left mouse button. Move the mouse up, down, left and right and the image will also move.

Except, the text may not act like you expect it to act.

There's a concept called text wrapping that controls where text that is near a picture behaves. If you've got the wrong setting on, you can move the mouse as much as you want but you won't get the visual appearance that you intend.

## How to Wrap Text around a picture.

When you click on an image to select it another line of icons is added to the taskbar.

There are three icons next to the phrase "Graphics" that control Text

Wrapping.  .

## *Wrap Off*

Clicking this icon means that text isn't put on either side of the image, but only above or below the image.

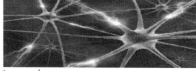

[1] This is a boring text document.

Nothing to see here.

## *Page Wrap*

Clicking this icon means that LibreOffice will place text both above, below, and either side of the image.

This is a boring text document.

Nothing  to see here.

### Wrap Through

The text will ignore the presence of the image. The text will disappear.

This is a boring text document.

Nothing

### Image Alignment

Just like text you can Align an image Left ⬚ , centre ⬚ or right ⬚ . You can find these icons next to the wrap icons.

Note, changing the Alignment of an image will also move the text if you've selected Page Wrap.

### What is an Anchor?

Click onto the image. You'll notice a symbol like ⚓ appear to the left or the right of the image. This is referred to as an Anchor because - like a boat - the image will stay in the same place relative to the anchor.

This doesn't stop you moving the image - but it means that it controls what happens when you change something above the image in the document.

## Anchor an Image to the Page.

If you want the image to just remain at the same place on a page you should Anchor the Image to the Page.

Select the image, then click on ⚓ ▾ . You will see a list of Anchor options:

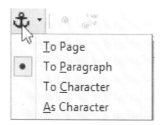

Click on To Page. Notice the Anchor goes to the left hand corner of the page. You can still move the image about, and resize it in the normal way. But when you type text above, at the side of, or below the image it doesn't move.

It's fixed to the same place on the page regardless of what other changes you make - at least, until you move it manually.

## Anchor an Image to a Paragraph

Click on the Anchor icon and click on ⚓ To Paragraph . Notice that the Anchor icon moves to the left hand side of a paragraph (normally the nearest one to the top of the image).

⚓re is a paragraph icon

You can move the image manually as normal, but an interesting thing happens when you add a paragraph above "Here is a paragraph icon". The image shifts down with the paragraph!

I added a line

Here is a paragraph icon

There's another interesting thing. You can move the image as normal, but if you left click on the Anchor and move it up or down to another paragraph the image also moves.

Added a line

Here is a paragraph icon

### Anchor To a Character

Selecting  To Character  is very similar to Anchoring To a Paragraph. Instead of anchoring to the start of the paragraph you anchor to a particular letter in the Paragraph. If you were click in front of the character and press enter the image would shift down with the character, but if you click below the character and press enter that character would remain in the same place and so would the image.

### Top, Centre and Bottom.

In the same way you can use Alignment to control whether the image is to the left, in the middle or to the right of the document, you can use Top, Centre and Bottom to control where the image is relative to your anchor.

First, anchor your image to a paragraph or character in the document:

⚓re is my achor

Look in the taskbar, and select the icon for Centre

⚓re is my achor

Notice that the image has moved so the middle point of the width is at

the same height as the anchor. If you click on Top ⬚ the top of the image moves to the anchor.

re is my achor

If you select Bottom then the bottom of the image moves so the bottom edge is lined up with the anchor.

re is my achor

Of course, these functions work whatever kind of anchoring you're using. For example, if you want to centre the image in the page, or put it to the top or the bottom of the page all you'd need to do would be to anchor the image to the page and select Top, Centre, or Bottom.

### How to Resize an Image

Putting an image on a page is quite a fun thing to do but sometimes the image may be too large or too small. Resizing your image is easy - but with one caveat. If you increase the size of an image you're not increasing the amount of data that your image contains - the computer only knows so much about the picture. Which means that as you increase the size of an image the quality of the image can go down - the jargon is that the image can "pixelate" - until it just looks bad.

Most people recommend that you avoid increasing the size of an image.

So, how do you resize the image? First, select an image by clicking on it:

Notice that on each corner and in the middle of each edge there is a small green square:

Click on one of the squares on the corners of the image and hold it down. Move the mouse diagonally towards the centre of the image to decrease the size, or away from the centre of the image to increase the size.

Notice that moving the mouse towards the top of the document will increase or decrease the height, and moving it towards the edge of the document will increase or decrease the width.

### Resizing the image without changing the ratio of length to width.

If you're not careful, resizing an image can affect the ratio of the images length to width. This can make an image look awfully funny:

For example, it can make people look very fat or thin!

If you want to resize an image while maintaining the aspect ratio (i.e. the ratio of length to width) this is slightly harder in LibreOffice Writer than some other word processors.

Right click on the image, and select Picture... . You will see the picture dialogue:

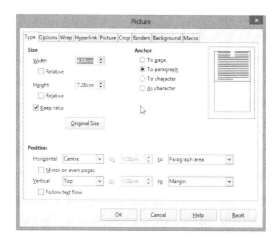

If keep Ratio isn't checked ☐ Keep ratio then click on the box
☑ Keep ratio .

In the Size section either use the arrows to increase or decrease the size

⬆⬇ or type the size you want into the box 4.25cm ⬆⬇ . Notice that
when you change one box the other box will change automatically as
well to keep the aspect ratio the same. When you're happy with the

size, click OK .

## Flipping the Image

Flipping an image involves either turning it upside down (flip Vertically)
or so that the left side is on the right (Flip Horizontally).

First select the image. Then, in the Format menu hover the mouse over
flip, and click either Flip Vertically or Flip Horizontally as appropriate.

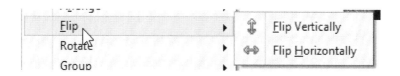

Clicking it again will return it to the original image.

### Rotating the Image

Rotating an image involves turning it 90 degrees to the left or right.

First, select the image. Then, in the Format menu hover the mouse over Rotate, and choose which direction to rotate it.

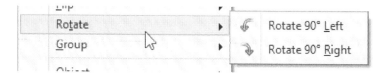

If you rotate the image four times it will return to the original image!

### Working with more than One Image.

It's possible to have two images overlapping. If you insert two images into the document and move one of them over the other, one image will "override" the other:

Imagine that both images are layers, and one is on top of the other. LibreOffice writer allows you to send one of these layers back, so that it doesn't show, simply select the picture you want to send to back and

click on the send to back icon: . Sometimes you might want an image to show, in which case you'd select the image and click on the bring to

front icon: ▢ .

## Compress an Image

Large images can take up a lot of space in a document. Often you can reduce the resolution of an image without sacrificing quality. Right click on the image, and select    Compress Graphic...    . LibreOffice will show the compress image dialogue:

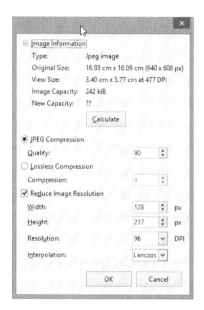

I recommend that you use the JPEG Compression method, simply type the quality in as a percentage. I.e. the finished resolution in the example below will be 75% of the original quality:

Then press OK. Take a careful look at the picture. If the quality has been reduced too much, go to the Edit menu and click on ↩ Undo: Apply attributes  Ctrl+Z  . It's important to do this before making any further changes since LibreOffice isn't guaranteed to store the original image for long.

## Caption an Image

You can give an image a caption by right clicking on it and selecting 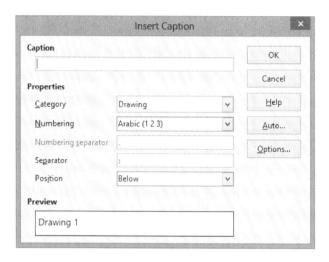 Caption... .

The Caption dialogue will appear:

Type the caption you want in the Caption box:

You can also change the following properties:

**Category** Whether the image is a drawing, illustration, chart

**Numbering** The number format

**Position** Whether you want the caption above or below the image.

Options... gives you the ability to control the caption style and borders.

Next Chapter

In this chapter we've covered images: how to insert, resize, caption and control their location. With what you've learned so far you're well on the way to making a document that looks great.

The next chapter will describe how to use LibreOffice Writers drawing capabilities.

# 6 IMPROVE THE LOOK

LibreOffice offers several functions that allow you to improve the look of documents, and even produce specialist forms of documents such as flowcharts.

While it'll never be as powerful as a fully specified drawing tool, you can certainly improve the look of your document. In this chapter I'll tell you:

- How to use standard clip art
- How to draw and use shapes
- How to write text vertically in the document and
- How to make some shapes 3D

## How to use standard clip art / the Gallery

The gallery has some standard clip art that may be useful when you

want to spice up a document. To access it press the Gallery Icon to display the Gallery dialogue:

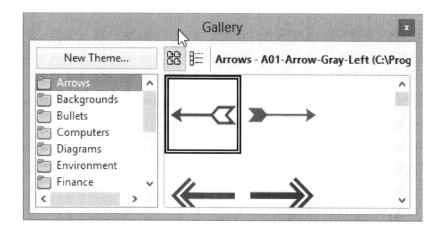

This is separated into themes such as Arrows, and the images stored in the Gallery (in the above case, an arrow).

Scroll down in the list of themes until clicking on the one that you want:

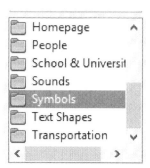

You'll see images in the box on the right of the themes, right click on the image that you want to insert:

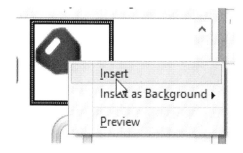

You can insert the item in which case it acts like an image you inserted from a file.

Another alternative is to Insert as Background:

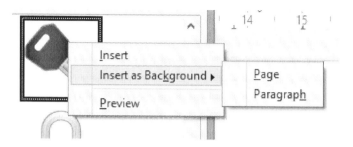

If you select the Page option you get the picture repeated throughout the page. If you select paragraph, it's only shown where you've written something. I don't recommend selecting paragraph as in my opinion it doesn't look brilliant but you can try it out yourself.

Notice that when you insert as background it acts like a watermark, so you can type text normally on top of the image:

### How to use shapes

Shapes can be squares, text, callouts, pie charts and any number of other objects which are used to improve the look of documents.

The draw functions are generally at the bottom left hand of the text window:

But sometimes you might not see them since it's possible to suppress them in LibreOffice. If you don't see them press the Show Draw icon ▨ in the taskbar.

| Icon | Icon Name | Description |
|---|---|---|
| | Select | Select items in drawing |
| | Line | Add a straight line to a drawing |
| | Rectangle | Add a rectangle to a drawing; the rectangle can be filled |
| | Ellipse | Add an ellipse to a drawing; the ellipse can be filled with a colour |
| | Free-from line | Add a free-form (i.e. wiggly) line to a drawing |
| | Text | Add text |
| | Callouts | Add a callout - something used to label or bring attention to a part of a drawing. |
| | Basic Shapes | Used to insert basic shapes like triangles, squares and donuts in the drawing. |
| | Symbol Shapes | Add symbols like square brackets into the drawing. |
| | Block Arrows | Add arrows to the drawing |
| | Flowcharts | Insert flowchart symbols into the drawing (a flow chart is a particular type of diagram) |

| | Callouts | Add one of many more elaborate callouts to the drawing |
|---|---|---|
| | Stars | Add a star to the drawing |
| | Points | Points allow you to resize, change the alignment or rotate an image. You've seen them before. This icon comes on automatically when you've selected a image. |
| | Fontwork Gallery | Examples of fontwork. Not advised. |
| | From File | Add an image from a file. |
| | Extrusion On/Off | Switched 3D effect on for image. When you put on Extrusion you'll see a number of other icons added to the draw bar. |

## Insert a Line

Inserting a line is simple. You click on the line icon, ╱ , press and hold the left mouse button at the place on the page you want the line to start, move the mouse to the end of the line and let go.

But, after you've done that you see some interesting new icons on the taskbar:

### *To make the line into an arrow*

Click on the ˅ next to ⇇ to show a list of arrows:

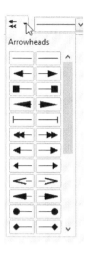

and click on the arrowhead style that you want.

*Change the style, and size of the line*

Next to the Arrow icon there are boxes to determine the line style (1) and Line width (2).

To change the line style(icon 1) click on it, and you will see a list of possible line styles.

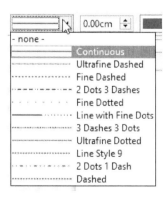

Click on the one you want. You can also change the width by clicking on

2 and typing in a width, 2.00cm or clicking on the up (to increase the width) ▲ or down ▼ arrows.

## Change the colour of the line

Next to the width box is the Line Colour box . Click on it to show the colour selection dialogue and click on the colour you want.

## Send line to Background / Foreground
The area that you type on is the Foreground. Sending something to the background means that you can still see it but you can also type over it.

Click on the Send to Background icon to send an image to the background.

If you want to promote the image to the Foreground, press  .

## Some other thoughts
Things like lines, rectangles, and other shapes are images in LibreOffice so the methods I've already shown you when we were dealing with images such as how to rotate, resize, and wrap work in the same way I've described earlier.

I don't want to bore you by repeatedly describing the same action; in the descriptions below it's assumed that things that are common behaviour for shapes will work as you expect it unless I specify otherwise.

## Rectangles
Press the rectangle icon and move your mouse to the top left of

the new rectangle. Press and hold the mouse button down, then move diagonally to the bottom right of the rectangle.

A rectangle can be divided into a line (i.e. the border around the rectangle) and an fillable area (i.e. the solid colour inside the line).

You've already seen how to change the thickness, style and colour of a line. You can use these options on the rectangle too, for e.g.

produces:

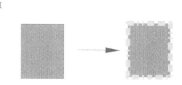

*Changing the Fill style and Fill colour of the area*
You'll find the Area Style (1) and Filling (2) next to Line Colour on the taskbar.

Click on Area Style(1) to select whether you want to fill the area with colour, a gradient, hatching or a bitmap.

Once you've selected that, click on Filling (2) to chose the filling you want, for example

would produce the following box:

It's worth playing around with the options to see what's available.

### *Adding Text to a shape*

You'll often want to add text to a shape. Simply double click on the centre of the shape, and enter in your text. Once you've finished, click off the Rectangle (i.e. on an empty spot elsewhere on the document).You'll quickly notice that there's something odd about it:

then Right click on the rectangle, and select Text:

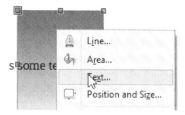

In the Text Dialogue you will see an option to Adjust to contour. Click it.

Then select OK.

When you're editing text you will see that the draw icons have been replaced by text icons in the taskbar. You can change font, size, add emphasis italics and bold just like normal:

### Insert a Ellipse

Insert an ellipse by clicking on the Ellipse icon ⬤ and then move your mouse to the top right hand corner of an imaginary rectangle surrounding your ellipse. Click and hold the mouse, moving it to the bottom right hand corner.

### Select multiple Images

So far I've ignored one icon. The Select icon. ⌖ . This is used to select multiple images. Click on it, then move your mouse to the top left of an imaginary rectangle that contains all the images you want to select. Click and hold the mouse down. Move the mouse to the bottom left corner of the rectangle. Notice that you see LibreOffice drawing a rectangle on the screen:

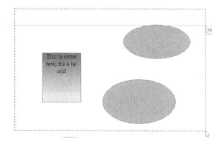

When you let go of the mouse the Rectangle disappears, but all the images completely inside the rectangle have been selected:

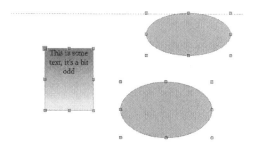

When several images are selected you can move them all at the same time.

## Grouping multiple images

It's possible to combine multiple images so they act like they are all one image - in other words you can move them, resize them, anchor them, wrap text around them instead of having to treat each image separately.

Once you've selected all the images (see above) right click on one and select Group

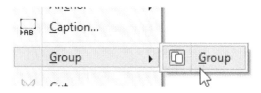

If you want to split the group apart again, right click and select Ungroup.

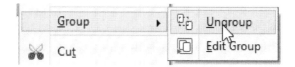

Sometimes you may want to edit an item in the group individually, but not lose the fact it's in a group once you've finished editing it. Select Edit Group. Once you've edited the group, click off somewhere empty in the document.

## Free Form Line

If you want to make a wriggly line LibreOffice has a tool just for you.

Click on the Free Form Line icon and move the mouse to the beginning of the line you're drawing. Click and hold down the mouse, then draw the line you want. Let go when you've finished.

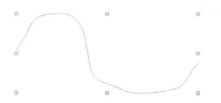

If you want to edit the path of the line click on the Points icon . You will see the line now has points all the way along it:

If you click on one of the points you will see two circle either side of a black square:

If you click on and move the Black square the actual path of the line will change between the adjacent two rectangles making a large change:

If you click and move the circle, you only affect the line between two rectangles:

### Text

It may seem odd that LibreOffice Writer offers a text icon in the Draw bar. While you can use text anywhere in the document, the text icon actually creates a text box that is very useful in illustrations. The reason for this is that although you can edit the text as normal, the box itself behaves like a shape.

You can anchor, resize, move and wrap text around the box as well as change its' colour.

To insert a Text Box click on the text box icon **T** and draw it onto the screen in the same way you draw a rectangle. Then type the text you want.

When you are editing the text you have access to all the normal text options such as font size, bold etc. But if you click on the border of the box, you get the draw / shape icons in the taskbar such as line thickness and style.

This is some wrapped text This is the text box       which goes around the text box like it's an image

## Callouts

If you want to draw attention to something you can use a callout. To insert a callout click on the callout icon ⌐ . Click the point you want to draw attention to(1), then move the mouse to the place you want to put the callout text (2). Let go. Click onto the callout text box(2) and type in the text you want.

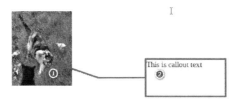

When you have clicked onto the callout text you'll have the normal options such as arrow, width, line style etc. I like to give my callouts an arrow and increase the width of the box.

## How to Write Text Vertically

There are many draw options that you can't see on the default draw toolbar. Look to the right of the draw toolbar and you'll see a little bar. If you hover your mouse over the bar the cursor will change to a little

cross ✛ . Right click on it.

Click on the Vertical Text icon (1) and draw the text box just like any other text box. The only difference is the orientation: it goes down the screen rather than across:

## Shapes

LibreOffice allows you to add a lot of shapes into a diagram. Shapes are pre-created draw objects that you can use to improve the look of you document. We've already described some basic shapes - rectangles and ellipses.

LibreOffice offers several categories of shapes on the draw toolbox by default including Basic Shapes(1), Symbol Shapes (2), Block Arrows (3), Flowchart (4), callouts (5) and stars (6). Your installation of LibreOffice may have different icons on the toolbar. This is because it's possible to add or remove categories from the toolbar.

You can see shapes that are less commonly used by right clicking the bar on the left of the draw toolbox and then hovering your mouse over Visible Buttons. You will see a list of icons; some are highlighted out, some aren't. If you click on a type of shape that is not highlighted you'll see that type of shape appear in the draw toolbar. If you click on a type of shape that is highlighted it'll disappear from the draw toolbar.

In the above diagram clicking on Free-Form line would remove it from the draw toolbar. Clicking on Curve would add it to the draw toolbar.

Once you've added the class of shape you want to the draw toolbar (if it isn't there already!) you can choose to insert the default form of that shape by clicking on its icon. For example, for the basic block arrow click on . You draw the shape onto the screen in the same way you'd draw a text box or callout.

Sometimes there are multiple versions of a shape. You can tell that there are variations available because there will be a down arrow next

next to the icon for the shape type you want. Click on it to select a variation. For example, to choose a variation of a block arrow click on

.You'll see a large gallery of block arrows to choose from:

Click on the type of block arrow that that you want. You can then insert it in the same way you'd insert a rectangle.

It's easy to add another arrow of the same type because LibreOffice changes the default to the most recently inserted variation of a shape. So, after I insert a right arrow, the block arrow item in the drawbar

changes to and you'd just hit the highlighted portion for another right arrow.

### Curves

If necessary add the Curves icon to the Draw Toolbar (see directions above). Click on it. To create a curve, move the mouse pointer to the start of the curve on the screen, click and hold the left mouse button. Move to the end of the line, let go of the mouse button. Now, move the mouse in the direction you want the image to curve. Double click when you're happy with the curve.

Note: It is possible to draw more than one curve or straight line at a time but I don't recommend doing this since it can be very temperamental. Instead, group a collection of lines and curves together to make the shape you want.

### Ellipse Pie

If necessary add the Ellipse Pie  icon to the Draw Toolbar (see directions in the shape section above). When you insert the Ellipse Pie you'll find that at first it's just like drawing an ellipse. But when you let go of the mouse button and move the mouse cursor into the ellipse you'll see a line.

Moving the mouse inside the ellipse also moves the line. Move it to the position you want the solid part of the ellipse to start, then left click. Move the mouse either clockwise or anticlockwise and you'll see a solid form with a gap in the centre.

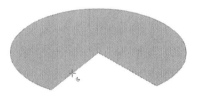

Moving the mouse cursor will move the edge of the solid part of the ellipse pie. Click again when you're happy that the solid portions is in the right place. If you've made a mistake and don't want to insert the Ellipse pie you've made click the right mouse button to cancel.

### Arc

Drawing an Arc is very similar to drawing an ellipse pie. You may have to add the arc icon to the draw toolbar (see instructions in the shape section above). At first, you draw an arc in the same way you'd draw an ellipse. Once you've let go of the mouse button, move into the centre of the ellipse. You'll see a line which shows where the beginning of the arc will be. Move the mouse until you're at the point you want to start the arc

When happy, click the left mouse button once, and move the mouse clockwise or anticlockwise to the end of the arc:

Click the mouse again when you are satisfied with the arc. If you don't want to go ahead with the arc, click the right mouse button to cancel.

## Polygons

If necessary add the polygon icon 🖱 to the Draw Toolbar (see shapes subsection above). Draw the first line in the same way as if you were adding a line, but you'll find that once you've drawn the line and let go LibreOffice Writer will automatically start drawing another line.

Move the mouse to the end of the second line and either click to start a new line, double click to finish adding to the polygon, or right click if you've made a mistake and don't want to insert a polygon after all.

## Making some shapes 3D

Sometimes you might want to make a shape 3D. While you can't do this to some drawing objects such as lines, arcs, or rectangles, LibreOffice does offer it for other types of shapes (including those from the basic shape gallery, ellipses gallery etc).

If you select a shape by left clicking it you'll see a greyed out Extrusion

On/Off icon if you can't add a 3D effect to that shape. If you can

add a 3D effect the Extrusion icon will be in full colour . Clicking on it will give the object a basic 3D effect but it'll also add some icons to the draw toolbar:

### Extrusion On/Off

Click this item to remove the 3d effect

### Tilt Icons

Click these to tilt the shape Down(1), Up(2), Left(3) and Right(4).

### Depth

Click this to change the depth of the 3d effect. LibreOffice shows a list of options. If one of them is OK for you click on it.

Otherwise, clicking on custom allows you to specify exactly how deep the 3d effect should be.

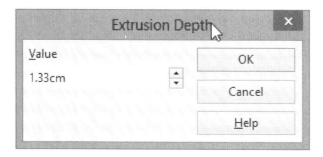

### Direction

Although you can control the direction of the 3D effect using the Tilt options described above there are some standard ways to display perspective available using the direction icon. Click on the one that you want:

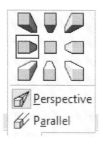

### Lighting

Depending on the Lighting direction your 3D effect will display shadows in different places. Click on the icon and it will show you a list of lighting directions:

Click on the bulb determine which is the brightest side of the object. You can also change how light or dim it is, although I recommend keeping this on normal.

### Surface

Click on this and you'll have the option of different surface types. In theory you can use this to change the look of the surface but the only one I find really changes much is the Wire Frame option which can be quite useful.

### 3D Colour

This allows you to change the colour of the 3D portion of the shape. When you click on it you'll see a colour selection dialogue. Pick one. You'll notice that the colour you've selected will be altered by the lighting option you chose above - so portions in shade will be lighter than the colour you selected, and portions in shadow will be darker:

## Next Chapter

In this chapter I've shown you how to use the Draw toolbar to add shapes, images, and adjust them. These functions - although not as sophisticated as a full desktop publishing program - allow you to make very nice looking documents.

The next chapter will show you how to use Styles and automated text to make your documents look more professional.

# 7 FONTS, STYLES AND TEXT

So far in this guide I've shown you how to do most of the Text basics, including how to change font and font size and use some basic formatting. But LibreOffice provides a large number of typesetting functions which allow you to have very sophisticated control of a document

In this chapter I'm going to show you:

- How to format Paragraphs and Characters
- How to automatically number paragraphs
- How to change the case of a section of text

While we've been doing pretty cool things with images it's great to come back to the main purpose of LibreOffice Writer - I'm sure you'll enjoy this chapter!

## How to format Characters

Formatting characters allows you to change the appearance of a selection of text. The first step is to highlight the text that you want to format. Go to the end of the text, click and hold the left mouse button, move the mouse to just in front of the text that you want to highlight:

It was the best of times, it was the worst of times, it was the age of wis
foolishness, it was the epoch of belief, it was the epoch of incredulity, i
the season of Darkness, it was the spring of hope, it was the winter of
before us, we had nothing before us, we were all going direct to Heave
other way – in short, the period was so far like the present period, that
insisted on its being received, for good or for evil, in the superlative de

Let go of the mouse and then click on Format-> Character

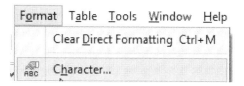

This will show the Character Formatting dialogue:

The dialogue has several features:

1: Font Name - type a font name in here if you know it.

2: Font List - A list of all fonts installed in the system. Click on one to use
that font.

3: Font Style - make a font Italic, Bold, or both.

4: Font Size - make a font larger or smaller. Fonts are listed in typesetting points.

5: Language - what language the section of text is written in. Useful when you're quoting someone who wrote in a different language than your main one.

6: Example of what the font choices you've made will look like.

7: Reset - returns all your font choices to the settings they were when you opened the Format Character dialogue.

So far, we've seen how to make all of these changes with other methods. But, notice that at the top of the dialogue there are some other tabs:

These tabs give you the ability to format the selection of text in a huge number of new ways.

1. Font Effects - Change the look of the text by making in embossed, or adding strikethrough or different types of lines.

2. Position - control what direction the text flows in, or whether the text is subscript or superscript

3. Hyperlink - make a link to a webpage or a file on your computer

4. Background - change the colour of the background, so your text appears highlighted.

5. Borders - give your text a border and control how that border appears.

## Font Effects
Go to the Font Effects tab and click on it.

This dialogue contains a lot of formatting options that are very useful.

## 1. Font Colour

Font colour

User

Click on this option to change the colour of the font.

## 2. Font Effects

Effects

(Without)

This allows you to choose what kind of capitalisation your text should have:

| Effect | Example |
|---|---|
| Without | n/a because your text will remain as it is. |
| Capitals | IT WAS THE SPRING OF HOPE |
| Lower Case | |
| Small Caps | |

| Titles | It Was The Spring Of Hope |
|--------|---------------------------|

It might be hard to see the difference between small caps and capital in a book; the difference is simply size.

## 3. Relief

Allows you to make the section of text embossed or engraved. I don't find that these options make a huge amount of difference in normal text and don't recommend them.

## 4. Overlining

Use these options to put a line over the text you've selected.

Note that there are a large number of options. In this example I've chosen Dotted (Bold)

It was the spring of hope.

Once you've selected an overline, you can choose a colour using the

Overline Colour option to the right

Note that under the Underlining box is an option Individual words which works on overline, strikethrough and underline selections to prevent them showing up in spaces between words.( e.g.

It was the spring of hope. )

### 5.Strikethrough

Strikethrough

(Without) ▾

Strike through allows you to put characters through ~~a piece of text~~ your selection.

You can choose from single (one line), double (two lines), Bold (a single bold line),  With / (~~It was the spring of hope~~ ) or With x (

~~It was the spring of hope~~ ) personally, I find that the single one line or bold options are generally best.

### 6. Underlining

Underlining

(Without) ▾

This allows you to select a variety of different styles of underline and works in the same way as the overline option above. You can select the Underline colour once you've chosen an Underline style.

### 9. Outline ☐ Outline

Changes the text from a solid block to an outline. e.g.

It was the spring of hope

### 10. Shadow ☐ Shadow

Puts a shadow under the text. I don't often use this option as I think that it doesn't really show up very well.

### 11. Blinking ☐ Blinking

This is used where you are working on a document that will mainly be read on the computer. It makes the text blink (i.e. it will flash on and off) which obviously doesn't show up when you print the document.

### 12. Hidden ☐ Hidden

Hides the text so it isn't visible. I don't recommend this option since it can be hard to find the hidden text again!

### More on the reset Button

When you make changes on a tab the reset button will put the settings back to the original ones for that tab. It won't affect changes you make on other tabs. So if you make a change to the font size, click on the Font

Effects tab, add an underline and then hit reset you'll go back to the original underline setting but your font size changes will remain unaffected. To reset the font size changes you'd have to click back onto the Font tab and hit the reset button.

## Position

The position tab allows you to select from options that control the position of text.

### *Subscript and superscript*

Position

○ Superscript      Raise/lower by    1%    ⬦    ☑ Automatic
◉ Normal          Relative font size  100%  ⬦
○ Subscript

Select ○ Superscript if you want to change the selected text to superscript (ie the th in $10^{th}$) or ○ Subscript to change the text to subscript ( the 8 in $O_8M$ ).

When you select either subscript or superscript you'll see that the greyed out options to raise/lower the font become active. Click on the square in ☑ Automatic if you want to be able to change how high or low the text is relative to the rest of the line. Then type in the percentage you want in the raise / lower by box or use the up and down arrows

Raise/lower by   66%   ⬦   ☐ Automatic . For example, the automatic setting leaves the text much lower than the 66% figure I selected earlier

$\_\_\_\underline{\text{spring}}\_\_\_$ vs $\_\_\overline{\text{spring}}\_\_$ .

You can also change the relative size of the supertext or subtext font by typing in the relative font size box: Relative font size  58%  ⬦ . The font size is calculated automatically based on the figure you enter, so your font (in this case) is only 58% as large as your standard font.

*Rotation*

You can make change the text so that it is rotated 90 degrees using ⊙ 90 degrees in the Rotation options.

the spring of hope

If you check the ☑ Fit to line option the text will automatically be reduced. I recommend only using this option if you are rotating one word at a time.

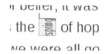

Using the ○ 270 degrees option will rotate it in the other direction spring .

⊙ 0 degrees will return it to normal. Scale width 100% ⬍ increases or decreases the width of the selected text e.g. the spring of hope, which can be a useful feature when typesetting. For example, if LibreOffice automatic spacing isn't working optimally you can slightly adjust the width of words so that you don't end up orphaned words at the end of a page.

*Spacing*

The spacing options allow you to control the number of points between letters in a word. Setting Default ▾ to expanded means that you'll be increasing the width between words, setting it to condensed means you'll decrease it. You set the amount of space in the by box

by 0.0pt ⬍ for example

produces the following text:

s the **s p r i n g** of hope.

I recommend that you keep  as it is. Pair Kerning adjusts the space between words slightly depending on the shape of the words. It's very subtle but it does make the document look far better in my opinion.

## Hyperlink

You can use the hyperlink tab to create a link to a website, to a file on your computer or to another part of your document.

### *Make a link to a webpage*

Type the URL / web address of the place you want LibreOffice to link to:

If necessary you can also select the target frame, but this is very rarely used in practise.

I suggest that you also change the character styles for visited link and unvisited link to internet link since this gives the user a visual clue as to the purpose of the link:

**Character styles**

Visited links | Internet Link
Unvisited links | Internet Link

When you click OK the link will be created in the document. Hold control and left click on the link to open the webpage.

### *Make a link to a document on your computer*

In the hyperlink tab click on the browse button  an open file dialogue will display. Select the file that you want.

URL  file:///C:/Users/Roy/Documents/Tom/NEA/Libre%20Office%  Browse...

Type in the name of the document

Name  Libre

Click OK. You'll see the link in the document. You follow it the same way that you'd follow a internet link.

### *Make a link to another place in your document.*
To make a link to another place in your document you first need to insert a bookmark.

Select the word you want to go to, for example in our document you might want to go to the first word. Then, in the insert menu select bookmark:

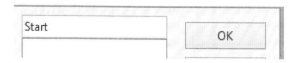

You will see the bookmark dialogue. Type in the name of the bookmark.

Start  OK

Then Press enter. Select the text where you want to make the link to your bookmark. Format->Character as normal and select the hyperlink tab.

In the URL field type the name of your bookmark with a # in front of it:

| URL | #Start |
| --- | --- |

You can edit the name and the link fields as normal but I suggest you leave them empty. Click OK. You'll see the link and you can follow it holding ctrl and clicking the mouse. When you're only dealing with text a few paragraphs away the effect isn't completely obvious - all you'll see is the cursor move. But if you're linking to another page then you see the effect more clearly. Your cursor screen will go to the bookmarked text wherever it is on the document.

### Background
The Background tab is used to select colours. It's just a colour selection dialogue, in effect. When you select a colour and ok the background colour of the text changes:

it was the spring of hope, it wa

It does the same thing as the highlight icon in the taskbar.

### Borders
The Borders tab is used to change the border around a section of text. You use it like a border dialogue. When you select a border and ok the text changes:

JI belief, it was the epoc

; the spring of hope, it \

are us, we were all goin

### Styles
So far I've shown you some basic ways to change fonts but it's often important to keep a level of consistency in a document. One way to do this is to have styles. For example, in this document the word Styles

above is in a predefined style called 'Heading 3'. I use this style for a particular type of subheading. I use 'Heading 1' for chapter headings.

While I'll go into a lot of detail later on, the thing to remember is that each style is rendered in a specific way. If you tell LibreOffice to change something about the way 'Heading 1' looks then it will change throughout the document.

You can change the style of a section of text by selecting the text, and clicking on the Apply Style list in the font icons (it's at the far left, next to the font name).

Chose the style that you want to selected text to be.

For example, you might want to change the text "A tale of Two Cities" from body text into Title.

In which you'd select Title in the Apply Style box:

And see the text change appearance automatically:

# A tale of two cities

S the best of times, it was the worst of times, it was the age of wisdom, it was the ;

Obviously there are a lot of other options you can use when working with styles. I'll describe them later but to understand some of the features in the Format Paragraph dialogue it is helpful to know that a style is simply a predefined appetence for a particular type of text and that if you change the settings for a style it affects all instances of that style.

## How to format Paragraphs

Formatting paragraphs allows you to control the flow of text, appearance of paragraphs, alignment of text and several other features. Where formatting characters controls the appearance of words on the page, formatting paragraphs controls how paragraphs appear in the document.

To format paragraphs select Paragraph in the Format Menu

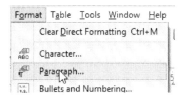

*Note: When you're formatting paragraphs by default you just format the paragraph where the cursor is unless you've highlighted more than one paragraph. If you've selected / highlighted multiple paragraphs then the changes will happen to all paragraphs selected. (If you have highlighted any part of a paragraph then, as far as format paragraphs is concerned, you've selected that paragraph).*

*If you want to make changes to the entire document press ctrl and A at the same time to select all, or go to Select All in the Edit menu.*

After you've selected format paragraph you'll see a dialogue. In the same way as Format Character has a lot of options you'll see that at the top of the dialogue there are a lot of tabs!

1: Outline & Numbering - lawyers and anyone who writes large documents sometimes choose to number paragraphs for ease of reference. This tab allows you to do that.

2: Tabs - Allows you to control how tabs are displayed. I won't describe these options since they are not useful for most people unless they are writing in Asian languages.

3: Drop Caps - Ever noticed how the first word in a book often has a capital letter that covers more than one line? Your LibreOffice Writer document can as well!

4: Borders - Control borders around a paragraph.

5: Background - add a background colour to an entire paragraph.

6: Indents & Spacing - It's bad practice to indent using the tab key on the keyboard since during editing it can leave random gaps      in the middle of lines. Tabs allows you to automatically set indentation so LibreOffice handles it for you.

7: Alignment - I've already showed you the basics of controlling text alignment, but this tab gives you some extra control which you might find nifty.

8: Text Flow - Allows you to control a number of cool typesetting options including orphans and widows as well as how hyphenation works.

## Outlines and Numbering

Outlines are useful if you want to produce a document like a contract or report where certain heading styles or paragraphs are automatically numbered. For example, if you were writing a contract you might want every chapter numbered but you wouldn't want to have to change each paragraph number each time you added a new paragraph.

LibreOffice allows you to configure Outline and Number options that determine how styles or paragraphs are numbered.

Before we start I'd suggest that you don't format Outlines and Numbering for a document until you've finished working on the document. It often works better if you select the entire document with ctrl+A and then change the Outline and Numbering options in Paragraph. This is because I find that LibreOffice sometimes forgets how headings should be numbered.

The first thing you'll see in the Outline and numbering tab is the following:

Note that we can configure the Outline / Numbering for each style. In this case we're modifying Body text, but we can also modify (e.g.) Heading 1.

The Numbering Style box gives you a list of different numbering styles to choose from.

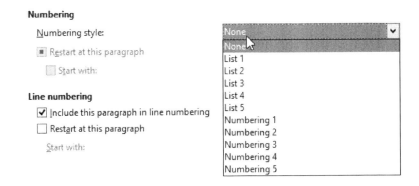

List styles are often in the forms of bullet points or letters, number styles are different forms of numbers. You'll have to experiment to chose the one that you want.

The next option in the numbering collection is restart at this paragraph. If you click this it will toggle the option off. ☐ means that the first paragraph of the section you've chosen won't be renumbered.

means the first paragraph that you've selected will be numbered 1 unless you toggle the Start With option on

in which case the paragraph will start at the number you've selected in the box I've highlighted above.

Line numbering is seldom used in practice but the options work in a similar way to the paragraph numbering options I've already described.

## drop caps

Drop caps are the larger capital letters often found at the start of book chapters. LibreOffice makes it easy to add these to a document. Highlight the section you want to make into drop caps (either the first word, the first letter, or first few words) and then click on Format->Paragraph and the Drop Caps tab.

To display drop caps click on the highlighted box: ☐ Display drop caps

When you do this the preview box will change to show you what the drop cap will look like

The next option controls whether it's the whole first word that is shown ☑ Whole word or a number of letters ☐ Whole word which you set in the Number of characters: |4| box.

You can control how many lines the of text the capital letter is dropped by. For example: Lines: |3| means the letter is dropped 3 lines:

You can put some extra space between the drop capital and the

'normal' letters using the space to text box.

Finally, you can set the drop caps to another style for example emphasis using the Character Style box

### Borders

The borders tab shows the same options as a Borders dialogue and acts in the same way. You can use it to set borders around paragraphs. The one difference between it and a Borders tab is the existence of the Merge with next paragraph option.

**Properties**

☐ Merge with next paragraph

Where you have two paragraphs that both have borders, if this option isn't set each border is rendered independently:

IT WAS the best of times, it w

it was the age of wisdom, it w
of incredulity, it was the seaso
was the winter of despair. we l

If you click on the box so it's set, ☑ Merge with next paragraph then the borders will merge together into one common border:

> IT WAS the best of times, it was the worst of times,
>
> it was the age of wisdom, it was the age of foolishness,
>
> of incredulity, it was the season of Light, it was the seas
>
> was the winter of despair, we had everything before us

The borders option can be useful if you want to draw a border around a particular paragraph to highlight it or a section of text.

### Background

The Background dialogue allows you to select the colour of the background in the same way as any other Colour Selection dialogue.

### Indents & Spacing

LibreOffice can automatically indent your text. While you can use the tab key to indent text it does it by putting a non-printing character into your work. This doesn't sound a bad thing, but the reality is that in a large document it's not too unusual for random orphaned tabs to appear during editing.

> If you want to indent a whole section of text, perhaps because you are doing a block quote, you can use the Before Text option below:

Although you can also highlight the text and click the increase indent  and decrease indent button on the toolbar.

The after text option puts an indentation AFTER the text, so for example

Would indent the text 2cm from the right border of the page:

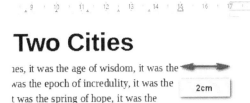

# Two Cities

les, it was the age of wisdom, it was the
was the epoch of incredulity, it was the
t was the spring of hope, it was the

2cm

The indent that we are most familiar with is the First Line indent. This is where we put a space at the beginning of every sentence:

First line:     0.50cm

Puts a 0.5cm space at the first line of every paragraph selected:

# A Ta

IT WAS the best of times, it wa
foolishness, it was the epoch of be
was the season of Darkness, it was

The Spacing options control how much space there is between different paragraphs. With Above Paragraph you're setting the amount of space above each paragraph Above paragraph: 0.00cm , in this example there is a 0cm gap ABOVE the paragraph. With Below Paragraph you're setting the gap below each paragraph. In this case I've set a huge gap to make it clear what's going on Below paragraph: 1.00cm . These settings will give you something like the following:

com

The
wen
it w
gen

i.e. a gap of 1cm between each paragraph. As a rule I recommend only setting one gap at a time, and I find a gap of 0.25 cm looks good in most circumstances . Also note that the gaps are appearing between different paragraphs of the same style. Sometimes, for example if you were using standard manuscript format, you might want to prevent these gaps happening. Toggle the following option

☐ Don't add space between paragraphs of the same style

by clicking on the square to prevent gaps between paragraphs of the same type.

There's another option called Line spacing. This is the gap between lines in the same paragraph. For example, it could be single spacing, double spacing (where you have a gap of an entire line), or as in the example below proportionate spacing:

**Single spacing** is the default option: it makes the line spacing a single line of text.

**1.5 Line Spacing** sets line spacing so there is an extra gap of half a line of text.

**Double spacing** sets line spacing to 2 lines of text, in other words there will be a gap of a line in between each line you write:

IT WAS the

foolishness,

**Proportionate Spacing** sets the spacing to a proportion of the line; so 120% will display the line plus 10% extra space above and below the line. Double spacing is equivalent to 200%, 1.5 spacing to 150%.

**At Least** can set the spacing between two lines of text of different fonts so you guarantee a minimum amount of line spacing

**Leading** sets the vertical space inserted between lines

**Fixed** sets the spacing to a specific number. This can result in cropping, because there might not be enough space on the line. I don't recommend this option.

While there are a lot of options available I find that I use single, double, and proportionate almost all of the time.

## *Alignment*

I won't discuss centre, left and right alignment - you can do these from the taskbar! This tab gets interesting when you justify a paragraph. You can set the alignment of the last line of the paragraph:

So, justification with the last line centre aligned would look like:

going direct the other way- in short, the period was so far like the present period, that some of its

noisiest authorities insisted on its being received, for good or for evil, in the superlative degree of

comparison only.

There were a king with a large jaw and a queen with a plain face, on the throne of England; there

If there is only on word in a line, the ☐ Expand single word expands the space between each letter until the word fills the entire line:

noisiest authorities insisted on its being received, for good or for evil, in the superlative degree

o               n               l               y             .

There were a king with a large jaw and a queen with a plain face, on the throne of England; there

## *Text Flow*

The text flow tab allows you to control typesetting features such as hyphenation of the final word of a sentence. By default, LibreOffice will not typeset the last word in a line so it is hyphenated. You can insert hyphens yourself or you can get LibreOffice to do it automatically.

To hyphenate automatically set the ☐ Automatically in the Text flow tab.

Changing the number in the ' 2 ⬍ Characters at end of line field controls the minimum number of characters left at the end of the line before a hyphen is inserted .Equally,

| 2 | ⏶⏷ | Characters at beginning of line

sets the number of letters that must be at the beginning of the new line. The combination of the two options means the word to be split must (in this example) be at least 4 letters long.

I don't recommend setting the break options in this tab: I think that it is much better to insert breaks manually.

### Next chapter

This chapter has shown you how to format characters and paragraphs to produce effective, professional looking documents. In the next chapter I'm going to show you how to edit text and how to use styles and templates to make the document look even better.

# 8 EDITING , RECORDING CHANGES, AND FIND AND REPLACE

In this chapter I'm going to discuss how to Edit a document, track changes, and how to find and replace text.

It will include

- How to move a section of text in the document,
- How to cut, copy and paste
- Making the document more than one column
- How to track changes you make to the document

## How to move a section of text in the document
Select the text that you want to move. Click and hold on the highlighted section with the mouse, and drag the cursor to where you want the text. Let go of the mouse.

You can often move other objects such as drawings in the same way.

## How to Copy
Copying text puts the text on the clipboard so you can paste it later. Select the text you want to copy then press ctrl and C or click on

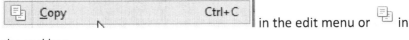 in the edit menu or in the taskbar.

## How to Cut

Cut text deletes the highlighted text after copying it to the clipboard. You can recover the deleted text by pasting it anywhere in the document. Select the text that you want to cut then press ctrl and X or

click on  or in the taskbar.

## How to Paste

Paste recovers the information you added to the clipboard. Go to the place you want to put the recovered text using the mouse. Press Ctrl

and V, or  in the edit menu

or in the taskbar.

## Paste Special

Sometimes you may want to paste something without copying the

formatting of the original segment of text. Click on the down arrow, and select unformatted text

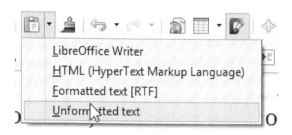

You'll notice that LibreOffice can include other options such as different file formats to use (i.e. RTF) all of which can provide slightly different looking formatting. In my experience it's rare to need to use these options but I often don't want to copy across the formatting.

## How to change the case of a section of text

Highlight the text whose case you want to change. Hover your mouse over Change Case in the Format menu. LibreOffice will show you a list of options.

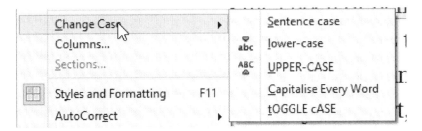

All of them are obvious except sentence case, which is the traditional English language sentence (i.e. a capitalised fist letter). If you choose tOGGLE cASE every capital letter will become lower case and vice versa:

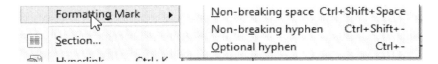

### How to insert typesetting characters

To insert a non-breaking space, non-breaking hyphen or optional hyphen hover your mouse over the Formatting Mark option in the insert menu.

I've already described how to get LibreOffice to automatically hyphenate but there may be circumstances where the ability to do this manually may come in handy.

### Insert Special Characters

Sometimes you may want to insert special punctuation, symbols, or drawings such as blocks. To insert these special characters go to the insert menu and click on Special Character

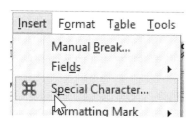

A special characters dialogue will be shown

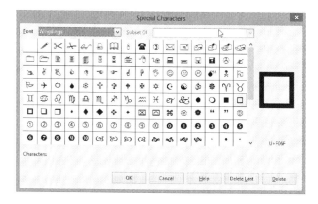

Note that you can choose a font. Often, one of the Wingdings fonts

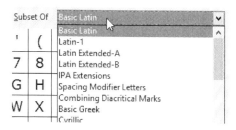can be very useful as they include

hundreds of different symbols.

There's also a Subset Of box which gives you dozens of options such as Basic greed, Latin, punctuation that can narrow your search down.

If you just want to add a single special character double click on it when you've found it. If you want to add multiple characters single click on the characters you want to add them to the Characters list:

119

If you change your mind and don't want to add the character click on

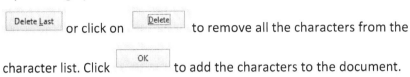 or click on to remove all the characters from the

character list. Click to add the characters to the document.

## How to insert Fields

LibreOffice provides the ability to automatically generate certain information like Date, Time and Author. It calls these automatically generated facts 'Fields', and it's easy to insert them into a document. Simply go to where you want the information to be inserted, then hover the mouse over Fields in the Insert menu and select the option you want.

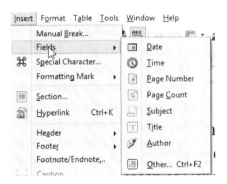

While LibreOffice Writer provides some automatically generated fields it also provides another type of field - a field that can be edited by the user. For example, if you were to generate a form for a user you might want to include a field for sex (Male / female).

These are available by selecting the Other option above or pressing Ctrl and Function Key 2 (F2) at the same time.

You'll see the Field dialogue:

Note that there are a number of field tabs including Cross-Reference, Functions, DocInformation, Variables, and Database.

I'll go into more detail about these later in the book.

For the moment, notice that if you click on a field type such as Date, you get the choice to select the type of date that you want. If you see (fixed) beside something, the date isn't automatically updated when you open the document. If you don't see it, LibreOffice will automatically update the field when it's appropriate to do so.

I'd also like to point out that in this dialogue you get a lot more control over the format of the field. There are dozens of options, giving you a lot of control over how the field is displayed:

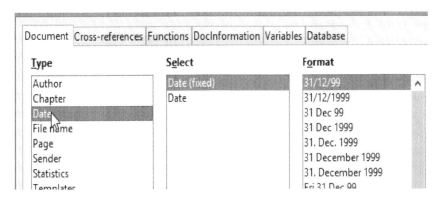

I'd also like to point out the DocInformation tab. Clicking on this provides you with a lot of information your operating system stores about the document, such as how long you've edited it

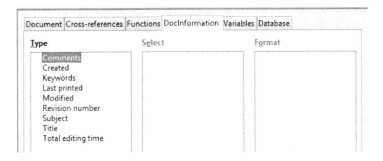

We've not covered much of this subject yet, but I promise I'll come back to it later on!

## How to Format the Page to Add Columns

You can either modify the entire page at once if you've not selected any text, or select an area of text where you want to add columns. Click

Columns... in the format menu to show the columns dialogue.

Set the columns dialogue to the number of columns you want, either by clicking on one of the pictures of the page layout OR changing the text box.

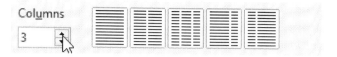

Check that you haven't made a mistake and you're applying the columns to either a section of text (if that's what you want) or the page.

The next option means that text you'll put the same amount of text into each column, otherwise the last column often ends up with much less text than the others.

☑ Evenly distribute contents to all columns

By default LibreOffice tends to make sure columns are the same width. If you toggle ☑ AutoWidth off, you'll be able to set the column widths yourself in the next series of options.

Generally, it does look better if you keep the widths the same throughout the document. With the settings we have so far our columns look like :

# A Tale of Two Cities

IT WAS the best of times, it was the worst of times, it was the age of wisdom, it was the age of foolishness, it was the epoch of

recently attained her five-and-twentieth blessed birthday, of whom a prophetic private in the Life Guards had heralded the

hands cut off, his tongue with pincers, and his bo burned alive, because he kneeled down in the rain

Personally, I like to add a little extra space between the columns using

Spacing

And a separator line between the columns

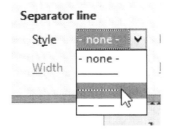

I think that this produces a better look overall, although people do have diffferent opinions about how much space and what type of line. You can change the colour and width of the seperator line as well.

# A Tale of Two Cities

IT WAS the best of times, it was the worst of times, it was the age of wisdom, it was the age of foolishness, it was the epoch of recently attained her five-and-twentieth blessed birthday, of whom a prophetic private in the Life Guards had heralded the hands cut off, his tongue torn out with pincers, and his body burned alive, because he had not kneeled down in the rain to do

## How to Track Changes you make

LibreOffice writer has a powerful proof writing tool that can be very useful when you're working on a team document. This is the track changes functionality. Everything that you change in a document is recorded, and then whoever owns the document can choose to accept the changes or reject them.

### Record Changes

In the Edit menu hover the mouse over Changes and click on Record

You've toggled Recording on ☑ Record . Clicking it again will toggle it off. This allows you to choose which changes you're recording.

When you make changes to the document you'll see the text that you've changed underlined in yellow.

IT WAS the best of times, it was the worst of
Inserted: Unknown Author - 28/07/2014 12:01
foolishness, it was the epoch of belief, it was the | it was the age of | going direct the other way- in short, the period | was so far like the present period, that some of its

we were all going direct to Heaven, we were all

Hover your mouse over the yellow and you'll see a tooltip saying who made the changes (if known) and when.

If you delete text you'll see the text go yellow, and have a strikethrough going right through it:

## ınd a ~~queen~~ with a

While recording LibreOffice will make sure that it remembers what you do so that someone can decide to undo the changes later.

### Making a comment about a change

Sometimes when a team is making a change it can be helpful to explain the reason so that whoever is responsible for accepting or rejecting the changes can understand why they were made.

Hover your mouse over changes in the edit menu, then select Comment... . You will see a comment dialogue box. Enter the comment in the text box and press OK.

[Note: See Accept or Reject changes further on in the book which explains how to read the comments]

### Protect Recordings

Where you are working on a document you may want to prevent

anyone accepting or rejecting changes without your permission. Hover your mouse over changes in the edit menu and then click on

Protect Records... . A password dialogue will be displayed.

Enter your password, then confirm it and press OK.

No one will be able to accept or reject changes unless they know the password.

This is more powerful than immediately apparent. Because you can use Protect Changes on a document before sending it to anyone any changes that they make are recorded and immediately obvious. It allows you to prevent anyone making changes to the document without your permission.

### Cycling through changes

To go to the next change hover over changes in the Edit menu and then select Next Change or to go backward in the document.

### Accept or Reject Changes

A simple option is to right click on a change, and select either

Accept Change or Reject Change from the list. You can also do the same thing from the Edit menu, by hovering your mouse changes and selecting those options.

However, I recommend hovering your mouse over changes and clicking on Accept or Reject... changes instead, since this will produce a dialogue with all the changes you've made, and the date and comment fields about why they changes were made:

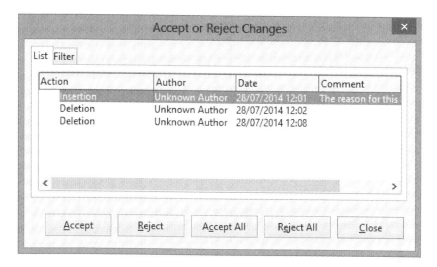

Double clicking on one of the changes on the list will move you to that change in the document so you can review it. Once you've decided it's as simple as clicking the Accept or Reject buton.

As a general rule it's unlikely that you will accept all or reject all changes but they're options that work as expected. When you've made all the changes you want select close to close the file.

### Compare Document

Sometimes you may want to compare two versions of the same file. To do this you need to click on

Compare Document...

in the edit menu. A file open dialogue will be displayed. Choose the file you want to compare the present document to.

If there are any differences they'll be treated as changes, underlined in yellow, and an Accept or Reject Changes will appear listing them:

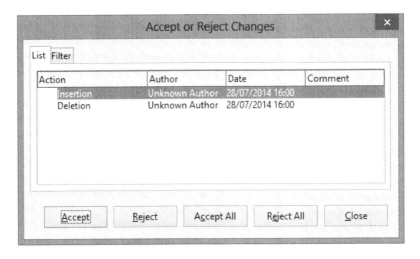

You can use the Accept or Reject changes dialogue in the normal way.

## How to Find Text

Sometime you may want to find a phrase or sentence. Press either

Ctrl+F or  in the Edit menu .

Just above the Draw Toolbar you'll see the Find Toolbar:

### Exist Search

Click this icon to close the Find toolbar.

### Search Phrase

Type in the phrase you are looking for here. Clicking on  will show a list of previous searches to choose from.

### Find Next ⌄ Find Previous ⌃

Click on Find Next ( the down arrow) to search forward in the document (in other words, towards the end of the document), or Find Previous to go backwards in the document (towards the front) from the present location of the cursor. If you don't find anything in the direction you're searching, LibreOffice will ask if you want to start at the other end of the document.

If there aren't any examples of the phrase, you'll see a message saying "Search Key Not Found."

### *Finding all instances of a phrase* Find All

Clicking on the Find All button will make LibreOffice go through the entire document and highlight every instance of the phrase. For example, if you were to search for it was, find all would do this:

> IT WAS the best of times, it was the worst of times, it was the age of wisdom, it was the age of foolishness, it was the epoch of belief, it was the epoch of incredulity, it was the season of Light, it was the season of Darkness, it was the spring of hope, it was the winter of despair, we had

It's very useful when you're looking for phrases you repeat very often.

### *Matching the case* ☐ Match Case

By default LibreOffice matches any combination of capital and lower case letters with any other combination. So it considers It Was and iT wAS as the same phrase.

If you want to search for phrases with the exact same capitalisation, toggle the Match case option on by clicking on the ☐ to make it look like ☑ Match Case . You can click on it again to turn Match Case off.

### How to Replace text

Sometimes you might decide that you want to change instances of a particular word to another one in your document. For example, if you were writing a book about Darren you might decide the name Danny might be better.

To Find and Replace text either press Ctrl+H or the find and replace icon .

This displays the Replace dialogue. You can type in your search text, then hit Find for the next instance of that search text. If you hit Find All, that will find all instances of the search text. I don't recommend doing that in this dialogue since it's better to decide whether to replace the text one phrase at a time - otherwise you might replace something that matches your search text by accident!

Put the text you want to replace in the Replace With box. Click Replace if you want to replace the text. Click Replace All if you want to change all instances of the phrase.

As in the Find Toolbar ☐ Match case restricts the results to those phrases with identical case. Toggling on ☐ Whole words only stops LibreOffice matching partial words. For example, Tom and Tomorrow  match with ☐ Whole words only toggled off, but with ☑ Whole words only toggled on they won't match.

Clicking on ⊞ Other Options gives you access to some other search options that are too advanced for this book but include things like registered expressions and searching for fonts.

## Next Chapter

In this chapter we've discussed how to Edit documents, how to find and replace text, and how to record changes so multiple people can work with a document.

In the next chapter I'm going to show you some tricks that help you to maintain a consistent look throughout your document.

# 9 STYLES AND AUTOMATED TEXT.

While it's nice to design documents on the fly if you run a business or write a lot it makes sense to do most of the design work once and then use it again and again.

Most professional designers agree that consistency is very important when making documents. Headings, body text, even quotations should all look the same throughout the document. Using styles it's possible to change the appearance of every quotation in the document, for example. This can also save a substantial amount of time as you modify a document.

This approach - maintaining consistency - is also very useful where you have text that you have to write again and again. For example, demand letters. In this chapter I'll describe how to use autotext.

### How to Use Styles

We've already said that it's possible to change the style of selected text from the text toolbar:

There is, however, a Style dockable window that gives you much more control over what styles you're using. You can modify the appearance of existing styles or add new styles.

Look on the right hand side of LibreOffice. The Style dockable window should look something like this:

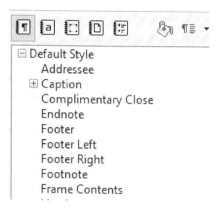

At the top of the Style dockable window are a collection of icons.

The first five of these icons relate to the type of style. The last icon allows you to modify or create new styles.

**Paragraph Styles** - Control styles like quotations, headers, and body text. Styles that are used in the paragraphs that you type.

**Character Styles** - Control styles like links, references, numbering, drop caps. Special character styles.

**Frame Styles** - Control the appearance of certain objects in frames.

**Page Styles** - Control styles associated with particular types of pages, such as title pages, first page, last page. So far we've only used a default page type. Now, we'll go into more detail.

**List Styles** - We've used lists and numbering before (in the

Formatting chapters). This is where we can change the appearance of list types.

**Fill Format Mode -** Used to 'paint' a style on a section of text.

**New Style from selection -** Used to create a new style or modify an existing one.

In addition to this there are a  list of styles below the icons:

This list will change depending on which of the first five icons you've selected. So, if you select the List Styles icon it'll be populated by list styles.

### How to change a selection of text to a style

Select the text that you want to change into a news style. Then, click on paragraph styles in the style dockable window. You'll see a list of available styles. Double click on your choice to change the selected text to that style.

When you are using a paragraph style like Heading 1, quotation etc you'll find that the entire paragraph updates if you select only part of it. Character styles will only affect the characters that you've selected.

### How to change the style of text using the Fill Format Mode

Click on paragraph styles in the style dockable window. Single click on the style that you want. Click on Fill Format Mode . Then, use the mouse as if you were going to select some text. The text that you select will automatically change to the font. Once you've changed the style of all the text you want to change I suggest that you click on fill format mode again  as otherwise when you select text or click on the text document you might find that the text style changes accidentally.

### *How to add a new style from a section of text*

If you change fonts in a section of text you may sometimes want to use those font choices again.

You have a choice between making it as a paragraph style where when you choose that style the entire paragraph will change to it or a character style where only the selected text will change to that style.

If you want to make a paragraph style make sure you that the paragraph style icon is highlighted. . If it isn't, click on it once.

If you want to make a character style the character style icon should be highlighted . Again, if it isn't - and you're not seeing character styles such as Numbering styles and bullets click on the character style icon.

Once you're in the right kind of style in the Style dockable window all you need to do is select the section of text where you've changed the formatting, then click on the down arrow next to the New Style from selection icon (I've highlighted it below). You'll have a list of options. Click on New Style from Selection.

You'll see a create style dialogue. Type the name you want to give the style in the Style Name box (in this example I've used the name Italic Emphasis). Click OK.

Note that if your section of text already matches the formatting of a style you'll see it appear on the list:

click OK, and the style will appear in the style dockable window ready for use:

Strong Emphasis
Emphasis
User Entry
Italic Emphasis
Footnote Characters
Page Number

## *How to modify an existing style*

In the style dockable window right click on the style that you want to change. (You may need to click on the paragraph style icon or character style icon depending what type of style it is). Click on modify:

You'll see a style dialogue. In this case we're editing a Character Style:

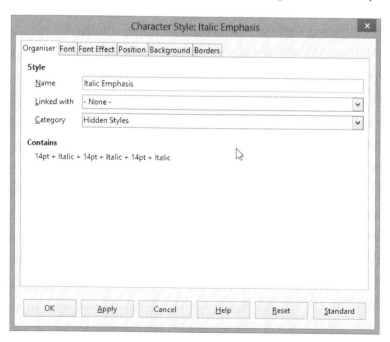

Font, Font Effects, Position, Background and Borders in the Character Style tabs are very standard. The Organizer tab is interesting.

Name is obviously the name of the font. Linked With gives you the option of deciding what the next font will be. So, if you were to select Linked With Text Body once you finished creating Italic Emphasis text by pressing enter, for example, LibreOffice would automatically set the next style to Text Body.

Categories Hidden Styles means that you won't see it when you're using the text styles box.

You can change the style to a custom style if you want to, or All.

### Page Style
This may be very controversial but I find that Page Styles are a good idea in theory but using them without causing problems is actually quite difficult in LibreOffice. Therefore, I'm going to suggest that you avoid them at this stage.

At a later date you may need to use them so that, for example, your left page and right page have different headers.

One of the biggest problem with Page Styles is that once you start to use them you need to make sure that changes you make in one Page Style are reflected in the other styles that you use - otherwise, you may end up with one style printing out an A4 document and another printing out as a A5.

### *Assigning a page to a style*
Click onto the page you want to assign to a style. Then, click on the page

styles icon and double click on the style you want that page to be.

NOTE: Some styles are linked. So, if you set the current page to be a left page, the next page will automatically set itself to right, and so on.

Apart from the Default page style which is the most common, there are three page styles that are often used:

- First Page; used as a chapter or section heading. May suppress headers and footers.
- Left page;
- Right Page

This allows you to do formatting commonly seen in books where the left hand page may have the book title, and the right hand page may have the author in the header.

*Modifying a Page style*
You can right click on the style that you want to edit and click modify. I don't recommend you modify page styles until you are very experienced with using LibreOffice.

How to Navigate
When you are working on a long document it can be hard to find a particular heading, table or chart that you want to go to. You can use the Navigator to travel around the document. Press function key 5 (F5)

OR click on the Navigator icon      in the taskbar.  You'll see the Navigator Window:

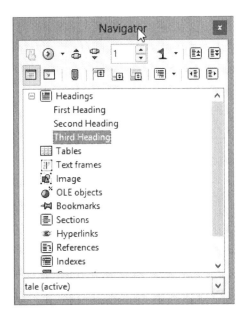

### Next and Previous

You can select what type of object you want to work with by clicking on

. You'll see a list of icons, and text (in this case, Headings). Hover your house over the icons until you find the one that you want.

You'll see the text change to whatever type of object you've chosen to navigate. In this case, headings.

Click on  to go to the previous instance of the type of object you're navigating (i.e. the previous heading) or to go to the instance of the type of object you're navigating (i.e. the next heading).

## *Moving Entire Sections of Text*

While working on Headings, you can move the heading around the document along with all the text associated with it (i.e. all the text until the next heading) by using the Promote ⬆ and Demote ⬇ chapter icon.

Promote moves the entire section earlier in the document so that it is in front of the previous heading of the same level.

Demote moves the entire section later in the document so that it goes behind the next header.

That's a bit of a mouthful, so maybe this example will make things clearer:

# Original Second Chapter

I used to be second, but I was promoted

# Original First Chapter

I used to be first

# Orginal Fourth Chapter

I was fourth

# Original Third Chapter

I used to be third, but I was demoted

## Small heading 2

When my major heading is moved, I move too

The above example has four Heading 1's. Promoting chapter two and demoting chapter 3 changes the order of the headings, and moves the associated text and any smaller headings in one go.

## *Going to a particular object*

The contents list is populated with object types, such as Headings. Notice that beside the object type there might be a plus sign (highlighted) which, when clicked expands the list.

Click the plus, to show a list of objects of that type

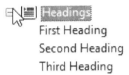

First Heading

Second Heading

Third Heading

If necessary scroll down to the item you want to go to. Then click it. You'll automatically move to the item you've selected.

*Promoting or Demoting a level.*

When we talk about Heading 1, Heading 2 etc we're talking about levels. A heading 1 is a higher level than level 2 - for example, a book might be divided into parts (header 1), Chapters (header 2) and sections (Header 3).

You can promote a header by clicking on it, then pressing (Promote level) . This would change a Heading 2 to a Heading 1. Demoting is done using the Demote Level icon .

Where an object type has levels you can promote it and demote it in the same way; obviously, there are other object types such as images which don't have levels. In that case the promote and demote icons are greyed out.

*Closing the navigation window*

Click on at the top right hand corner, or click on the taskbar to close the window. While I haven't described all the options I think that I've covered the most useful ones that you will use again and again. The ability to travel to particular places in the text, and also the ability to move entire sections of text around the document at will are very useful.

## Automated Text

Automated text allows you to store text that you use regularly so that you can put it in the document without typing it in again and again. It's useful because it reduces the number of transcription errors that you might experience.

### Inserting Automated text

Open the Automated Text window by selecting

AutoText...        Ctrl+F3   in the edit menu or pressing Ctrl+F3.

You'll see the AutoText window. Expand a category by clicking the plus in the box beside it. Double click on the automatic text you want to insert.

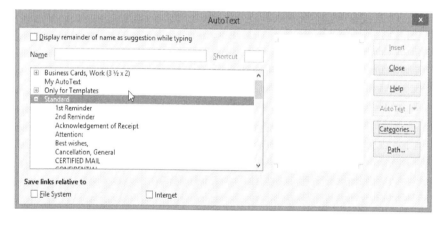

The window will disappear, and LibreOffice will have inserted the text into the document wherever you've left the cursor.

Many of the autotext examples have placeholders, e.g. the blue text between < and >

ny <SUBSCRIPTION OR SIMILAR.> at the

click on the text and change it to whatever is appropriate.

143

## Shortcuts with Autotext

Notice that there is a shortcut field which displays a combination of letters when you click on an autocorrect item.

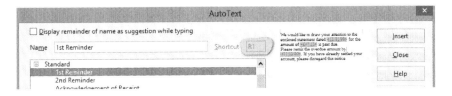

if you type this text and then press F3 the text is replaced by the autotext by LibreOffice. That's the reason that Autotext is such a powerful function.

For example, if you were to regularly type out your signature:


Yours sincerely


Thomas Ecclestone

Setting up a YS shortcut would mean you could put that text in with only three keystrokes.

### *Importing Autotext*

Unfortunately, adding autotext in LibreOffice can be a lot of a pain. In order to import autotext you need to make a word 97-2003 template file with autotext. And to do this you need a copy of word.

You'll also need to add a new custom path to the document.

STEP 1 - Creating autotext in word 2007

1.  Create a new document

In word 2007 press the 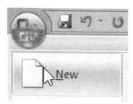 Office Button and click new:

Double click on Blank Document

2. Save document as a template

Word 2007 saves autotext in document templates. So, you need to save the file you're adding as a word template first. Hit the office button, hover the mouse over save as, then click word template.

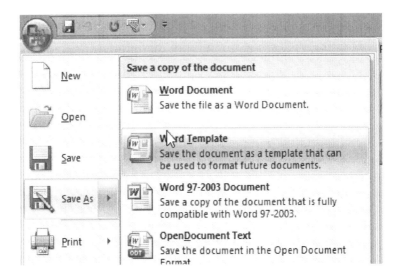

You'll see a normal Save As dialogue.

Choose the file location and file name first, in the normal way. It's important that you remember the path of the file for a later step.

Before saving, click on the down arrow by the save as type box

Select Word 97-2003 Template from the list. The Save as type box should look like:

When you're happy that you're saving the template to the right directory, with the right file name and file type, hit OK.

3. Add autotext

Type in the text that you want to add as autotext, and then select it in the same way you would in LibreOffice

This is some text that I want to add

Press Alt-F3 to bring up the building blocks dialogue

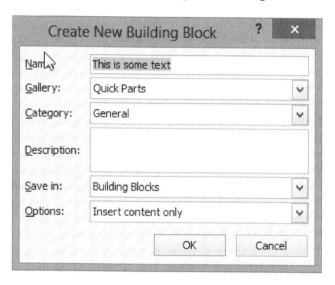

In LibreOffice there is a shortcut field which corresponds to the name field in Word. It's important that you change the Name to a shortcut you're willing to type a lot.

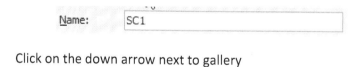

Click on the down arrow next to gallery

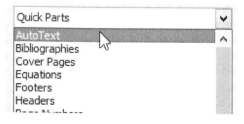

And select Autotext from the list:

finally, click the down arrow next to Save In

And choose the name of your template file from the list

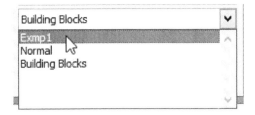

You'll end up with a dialogue that looks like:

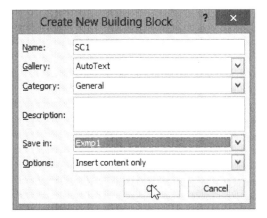

Although obviously the name and save in boxes will reflect your choices

Repeat this process as many times as you need, until you've got all the autotext items that you want.

4.  Save document

Press Ctrl+s to save the document. You may get a warning that says you may lose some formatting, in which case click OK.

Step 2 - Creating a Path in LibreOffice

5. Open the AutoText editor by hitting Ctrl+F3

6. Click on the **Path...** button

7. In the Path dialogue press Add **Add...**

8. Locate the directory you stored your template in ( the path) and click on it.

Then click on OK

9. You should see your path in Select Paths dialogue

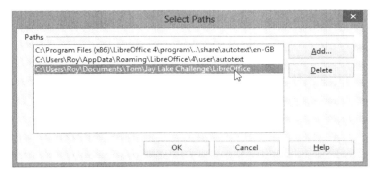

If you're happy, press OK. You can delete a path by selecting it and pressing Delete

Step 3 - Creating a category in LibreOffice

10. Hit the  button
11. You'll see the Edit Categories dialogue. Type in a name for a category in the Category box:

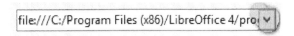

12. Click on the down arrow to the right of the Path Box

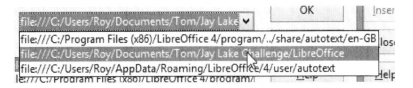

13. Click on the path you've just added in the Path List

14. Hit  .

Note that the category appears in the Autotext window:

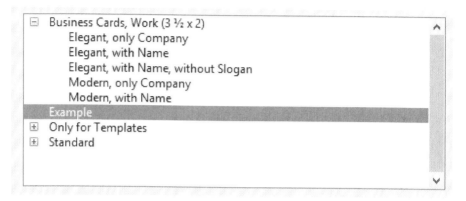

At this stage, though, the category doesn't have any actual autotext in it.

Step 4 - Importing Auto text

15. Click on the Category you've just created (in our example it's called Example)
16. Click on the Autotext button

17. Click on import

18. A Open file dialogue will appear. The first step is to click on the file type box next to the file name:

19. and click on Microsoft Word 97/2000/XP/2003 template

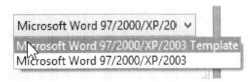

20. Then select the template we made earlier from the list of files

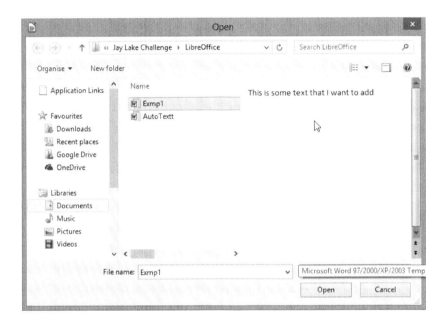

21. Press Open.

As if by magic, the autotext will appear in your new category.

Well, it's been quite a palaver hasn't it - but if you think about it by creating autotext you're saving yourself a lot of trouble having to repeatedly add the same text again and again.

## What are templates?

At its simplest, templates are standard documents which can be used again and again. For example, if you were to write a sales letter to new customers you could store it and then every time you needed the letter for a new customer all you'd have to do is create a new file from the template.

When you make a template your decisions about styles, designs, and even document text are all 'copied' and used in any new file you make from the template

### Creating a template

First, create a new file. Edit the style, design, and content of the file like any other document. Remember that you're going to use what you do again and again though so try to keep any wording general enough so you can use it without too much modification.

### *Inserting Placeholder Fields*

One way that you can make a document more customisable is to include Placeholder fields. For example, in a letter you might have customer name as a placeholder.

1. Highlight the text that you want to make into a placeholder field
2. Press Ctrl+F2
3. Click on the Variables tab

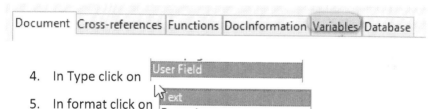

4. In Type click on [User Field]
5. In format click on [Text]
6. Type in a Name for the field:

7. Type in the text that will appear in the field in the value box

   then press enter of click ✔
8. Click on the field you've just added in the select list

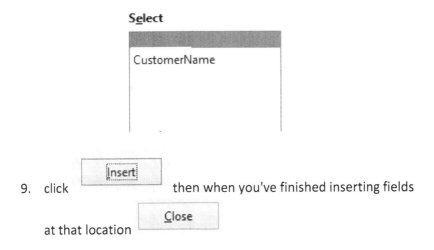

9. click **Insert** then when you've finished inserting fields

at that location **Close**

You'll see the new Placeholder field has been inserted at the cursor

Dear Enter Customer Name

To enter text into a placeholder click on it and start to type.

### Saving a template

Once you've finished editing the document to your satisfaction, hover your mouse over templates in the file menu, and click on save as template

Click on 🖥 Save

Type in a name for the template then click OK

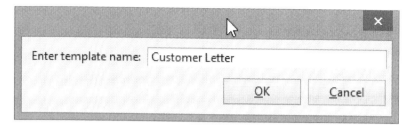

You'll see the new template in the template manager:

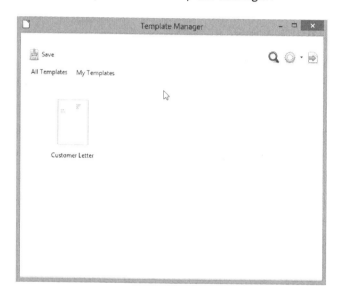

### Use a Template

To create a file from a template, hover your mouse over new in the file menu, and click on

You'll see the Template Manager. Just scroll to find the template you want to use and then double click on it.

LibreOffice will create a new file based on that template.

### Edit a Template

Hover your mouse over Templates in the File menu, and click on

Manage

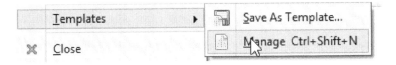

Scroll down to the template you want to edit, and click on it. Then click

on ![Edit icon] Edit . The template will open. Make sure that once you've finished editing it you save.

Note that changing a template will not change files that you made prior to editing it. It will only affect files that you make subsequent to the change.

### Remarks on premade Templates

You don't necessarily need to create your own template. By clicking the

![icon] icon in Template manager you'll open an browser window that opens on a LibreOffice site with hundreds of premade templates that you can use.

### Next Chapter

In this chapter I've shown you how to add and modify styles , templates, and autotext to help maintain a common look throughout a document.

Styles allow you to make sure that similar kinds of text looks the same all the way through the document. Autotext can be used to save time but also to make sure that you always use the same text in a specific circumstances.

Last but not least templates allow you to use the same formatting and design decisions as well as the same text on every instance of a document type.

In the next chapter I'll show you how to use some basic tables.

# 10 TABLES

At its simplest a table is a grid which can contain text, numbers or other objects. You often find them in books, for example

| Name | Sex |
|------|------|
| Joe | Male |
| Jane | Female |
| Fred | Male |
| Mark | Male |
| Sarah | Female |
| Mary | Male |

While that is their most common, tables can be quite handy when lining up images or text information on the page.

This chapter will only detail manually generated tables. It won't go into detail about the automatic tables such as tables of content and references which are very useful tools in themselves.

## Inserting a table
Hover over insert in the table menu, then click on table.

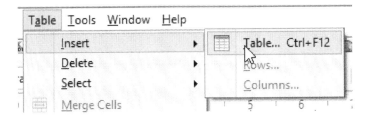

You'll see the insert table dialogue. First, enter a name for the table that you are creating.

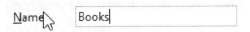

Enter in the number of columns you want

and the number of rows

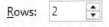

The above example will produce a table with three columns and two rows:

| Row 1 | Row 1 | Row 1 |
|---|---|---|
| Row 2 | Row 2 | Row 2 |

Note that rows go across the document (see above) and columns go down the document. The settings for row and columns are not critically important since I will show you how to insert and delete them later on.

The next field in the insert table dialogue is ☐ Heading . If you click in the square to toggle it on ☑ Heading , then LibreOffice will make the first row of the table visibly different to the others.

| Word | Description |
|---|---|
| Hat | Something you wear on your head |
| Map | Something you use to show your direction. |

When you've toggled the heading on, you can also choose to toggle on (by clicking in the square until it's got a tick in it) an option to repeat the header if your table goes onto a new page:

☑ Repeat Heading Rows on new pages

Heading Rows:   1   ⬍

The heading rows will normally be 1, but you could have more than one row used for the headers sometimes.

I generally suggest that you leave ☐ Don't split table over pages toggled of. If you were to toggle it on you'd stop the table splitting into the next page if there isn't enough space. Instead the entire table would move to the next page.

Until you've finished editing the table I suggest that you leave ☑ Border toggled on. This is because it makes it easier to resize the table.

Once you're happy click Insert .

## How to modify a cell

Each "square" inside the table is a cell.  In this example, there are 6 cells:

| | I am a cell |
|---|---|
| | |
| I am a cell | |

If you move over a cell and click the left mouse button the cursor will move to the cell and you will be able to start modifying the contents of the cell. Right clicking and selecting font, for example, will change the font in that square:

| | I am a cell |
|---|---|
| I edited tHe FoNt iN tHiS CeLL | |
| I am a cell | |

It's also possible to modify entire rows and columns at the same time; I'll explain how latter.

### Deleting a table

Put your mouse over any cell in the table. Hover over Delete in the Table menu, then select table.

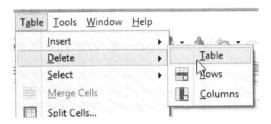

The entire table will be deleted.

### Selecting Rows and columns

To select a row either click into a cell in the row and hover your mouse over select in the Table menu and then click on Rows:

Or move your mouse just to the left of the first cell in the row that you want to select

until the mouse cursor changes to ➡ . Click once to select the row.

| | I am a cell |
|---|---|
| → I edited the Font in this Cell | |
| Select table row | |

Likewise, to select a column click into a cell in the column and hover your mouse over select in the table menu then click on Columns

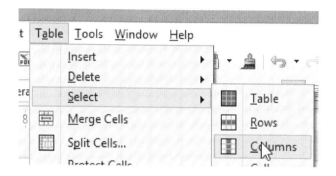

Or move your mouse just above the first cell in the column until the mouse cursor changes to ↓ and then click once.

| | Select table column a cell |
|---|---|
| I edited the Font in this Cell | |
| I am a cell | |

## Selecting a cell

To select multiple cells, go to the top left hand corner of the first cell in your selection, click and hold the mouse, then move the mouse cursor to the bottom right hand cell of your selection.

Selecting a single cell is more difficult with the mouse so I suggest clicking into the cell then hovering over select in the table menu and clicking on cells.

## Moving boundaries

Sometimes you may want to increase or decrease the width of a row or column. Slowly the mouse cursor over the boundary you want to move.

It will change from $I$ to

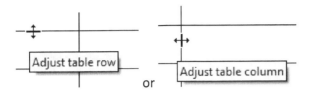

or

Click and hold the mouse button down. If you are adjusting a row, move the mouse up or down to change the location of the boundary. If you're adjusting a column move it left or right.

Note that sometimes LibreOffice Writer will be able to expand the size of the table to allow for changes you make to width or height but sometimes it won't and will have to use more lines of text and / or truncate the content of a cell which it can't display.

When moving boundaries you need to watch what happens to the entire table. It does require practise.

## Merging Cells

To merge two or more cells together first select the cells that you want to merge

| 1 | 2 | 3 |
| 4 | 5 | 6 |
| 7 | 8 | 9 |
| 10 | 11 | 12 |

Right click on the highlighted selection and hover your mouse over cell, then click merge

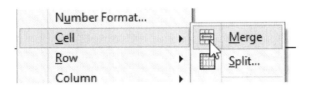

Note that the cell for 5 and 8 has merged together in the example below.

| 1 | 2 | 3 |
|---|---|---|
| 4 Select table row | 5 | 6 |
| 7 | 8 | 9 |
| 10 | 11 | 12 |

### Splitting a cell

Right click on the cell you want to split, hover your mouse over sell and click on split:

You'll see the Split Cells dialogue. You can chose how many cells to split the cell into

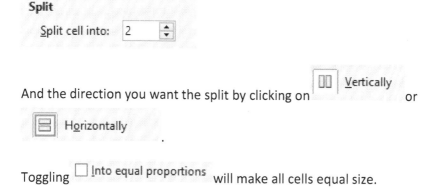

And the direction you want the split by clicking on Vertically or Horizontally.

Toggling Into equal proportions will make all cells equal size.

For example, if we split our example table above vertically we'd get:

| 1 | 2 | | 3 |
|---|---|---|---|
| 4 | 5 | New cell | 6 |
| 7 | 8 | Adjust table column | 9 |
| 10 | 11 | | 12 |

## Auto format a table

While a basic table is very functional, people often want a bit more glamour and design. While you can manually format a table so it's pretty LibreOffice provides a tool called Table autoformat which provides some great designs to liven up your document.

To use it simply click into any cell in the table.

Click on  in the tables menu.

You'll see a list of Formats(1) which offer lots of options. Click on one and it will be previewed in the preview window(2)

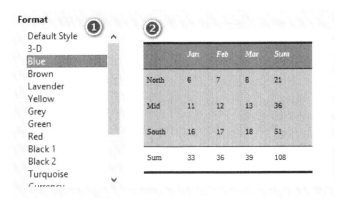

You can choose to stop LibreOffice changing some of the features of the table by toggling off the appropriate option in the Formatting part of the dialogue.

For example if you toggle off Font (i.e. click on the plus in the box beside

Font so it looks like 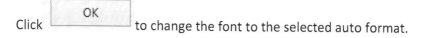 ) then LibreOffice won't change the fonts you're already using in the table.

Click  to change the font to the selected auto format.

## Formatting a column, row, cell or table manually

Select the cells that you want to format. Then, you'll find that you can format the selected cells either by right clicking on one of the highlighted cells and hovering your mouse over the correct option

Or choosing  one of the formatting options from the table taskbar  in the iconbar.

These options work pretty much as you would expect, for example

 changes the background colour.

## Number Format

The default number format isn't always the one that is most appropriate for the data that you're entering into a cell. For example you might want the numbers in your cell to have a certain number of decimal places or be a currency.

First, select the cells where you want to change the number format. Right click on the highlighted area, and then click on

.

The Format Number dialogue will appear. By default LibreOffice generally formats numbers as Text. But there are a lot of other categories you can choose from, for example percent or currency:

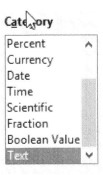

Choose the one that you want. Note that when you select a category you'll generally see options for that category appear in Format.

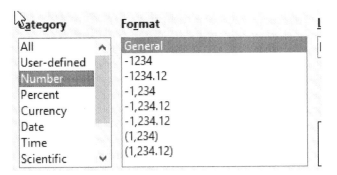

You'll see an example of what your choices will look like under the language box ( marked 1)

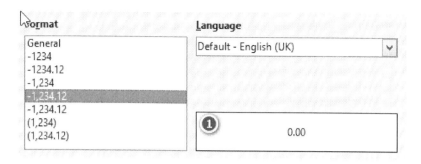

You can control other options related to your format and category choices, for example control the number of decimal places or parts. This changes slightly depending on what categories you've chosen.

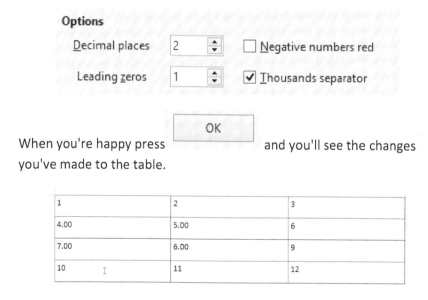

When you're happy press [OK] and you'll see the changes you've made to the table.

| 1 | 2 | 3 |
|---|---|---|
| 4.00 | 5.00 | 6 |
| 7.00 | 6.00 | 9 |
| 10 | 11 | 12 |

Obviously, there are a lot of different number formats that you can choose so you'll probably have to experiment to see which format is the best for your table. If you make a change that you aren't happy with use the undo to go back to how the table was before you changed it.

## Protecting cells

Sometimes you'll have a cell(s) where you want to prevent accidental changes. You can do this by selecting the cells you want to protect (upto and including rows, columns and tables), right clicking on the highlighted area, and hovering your mouse over cell. Then click protect.

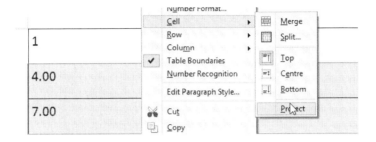

If you try to change the cell you will get a warning message

To remove the protection select the cells you want to unprotect, right click on the highlighted area, hover the mouse over cell and then click on unprotect.

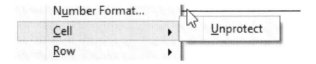

## Showing boundaries

If you combine changing the size of cells, merging them, splitting them together you quickly realise how powerful tables can be as a layout tool. You can make sure that drawing objects, text and so on all line up together and items are located exactly where you want them.

This becomes especially useful once you realise that you can make the borders of the table invisible - so, when you print out they just don't exist as far as the reader is concerned!

First, right click on any cell in the table and then click on.

<u>T</u>able...

You'll see the Table Format dialogue. Click on the  tab, then in Line Arrangement click on the clear borders option (highlighted)

**Line arrangement**

<u>D</u>efault

and press OK. You'll see the table change so it doesn't have any borders.

| 1 | 2 | 3 |
|---|---|---|
| 4.00 | 5.11 | 6 |
| 7.00 | 6.00 | 9 |
| 10 | 11 | 12 |

## Inserting a caption

Right click on any cell in the table and then click on

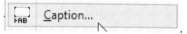 .

Type in the text you want for your caption:

**Caption**

This is my table

The default options are normally quite good, but if you want to change the numbering click on the down arrow :v

 and chose from the list.

You can also change the position of the caption

Once you're satisfied, click OK:

| 1 | 2 | 3 |
|---|---|---|
| 4.00 | 5.11 | 6 |
| 7.00 | 6.00 | 9 |
| 10 | 11 | 12 |

*Table 1: This is my table*

Note that the table number will automatically update if you insert or delete a table in the document.

### Table to Text

Converting a table to text is easy. Select the whole table. Hover the mouse over convert in the table menu, then click on table to text:

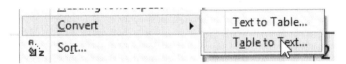

You'll see the table to text dialogue. You can chose what to use to separate text by, but I'd suggest keeping the default setting of tabs.

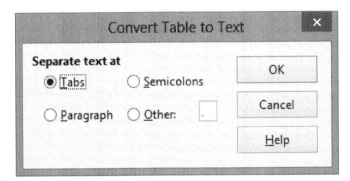

Click on OK.

### Next Chapter

In this chapter I've shown you some of the basics of how to use tables. Once you get a hang of them you start to find them very useful not just where you have large amount of text to display but also where you want a fine control of the location of items on a page.

In the next chapter I'm going to discuss how to handle references, tables of contents, and footnotes in LibreOffice.

# 11 TABLES OF CONTENT, INDEX, AND FOOTNOTES

When you are writing a large document the ability to insert Tables of Contents and indexes is very useful. This is especially true of reports and nonfiction books. Doing them manually is a chore and means that every time you edit the book you'll need to spend a long time changing these items. Fortunately, LibreOffice can automatically generate front and back matter for you. So all you need to do is spend your time concentrating on the content of your report!

In this chapter I'll discuss:

- How to automatically generate a table of content
- How to make an Index
- How to make a bibliography.
- How to generate footnotes and endnotes.

### How to insert a table of contents

It's important to know that generally a table of contents is automatically generated from heading styles. You can specify the number of levels in a table of contents - for example, you might want your table of contents to only list headings level 1 and 2.

So, before you start make sure that you are using Heading Styles throughout your document.

You can exclude a section header from the report by creating a new nonHeading style with the same format as the headings. You can do this by selecting the heading you don't want to include

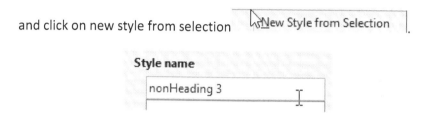

Clicking the new style from selection icon ¶≣ in the styles and formatting dockable window.

and click on new style from selection ↳New Style from Selection .

Click OK. Note that once you've created a nonHeading style for a heading level you don't need to create it again. Just select the heading you don't want to show up and then choose the new style from the

apply style list nonHeading 3 ⌄ .

I'd suggest that it is actually a good thing to wait to create your table of contents until the last moment - when you're happy that the document is completely finished and you've made all the correct style decisions.

Once you're happy go to the place you want to insert your table of contents.

Then hover your mouse over Indexes and tables in the insert menu, and click on Indexes and Tables.

You'll see the index and tables dialogue open

Make sure that you're on the  tab, (this is the default, but click on the Index/Table tab if the index and tables dialogue opens in another tab).

Check that you're creating a Table of Contents
Type [Table of Contents ▼]. If the type listbox doesn't show Table of Contents, click the down arrow and select it from the list.

You can change the name of the table in Title, but I'd suggest keeping it to the default table of contents

Title | Table of Contents

I think that it's generally a good idea to only update a table automatically.  but you can toggle this if you want to make changes yourself.

By default, LibreOffice creates the table of contents for the entire document. If you want to make the table of contents only for a particular chapter or section click the down arrow. This can be useful where your book or report is divided into parts.

**Create index/table**
for [Entire document ▼]

The next option allows you to limit the scope of the table of contents. These levels refer not to Heading Levels, but contents levels. We're going to set what styles are at a particular level later on.

Evaluate up to level [10 ▲▼]

As a general rule I don't suggest that you change this option.

It's important to specify the styles that you want to make into table of contents items: Click on the square next to Additional styles

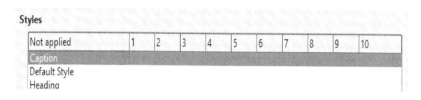

to toggle it on, then click on      to show an assigned styles dialogue.

Simply click on the non applied style you want to include in the list

| Styles | | | | | | | | | | |
|---|---|---|---|---|---|---|---|---|---|---|
| Not applied | 1 | 2 | 3 | 4 | 5 | 6 | 7 | 8 | 9 | 10 |
| Caption | | | | | | | | | | |
| Default Style | | | | | | | | | | |
| Heading | | | | | | | | | | |

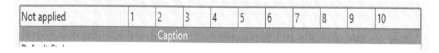

And then click on      to make the style move to a higher level on the list. I.e. clicking it once will make LibreOffice consider the style level 1, clicking it again will make it level 2

| Not applied | | 1 | 2 | 3 | 4 | 5 | 6 | 7 | 8 | 9 | 10 |
|---|---|---|---|---|---|---|---|---|---|---|---|
| | Caption | | | | | | | | | | |

If you want to make the style move to a lower level on the list click on

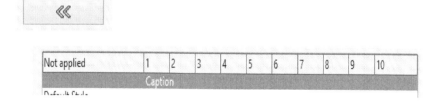

| Not applied | | 1 | 2 | 3 | 4 | 5 | 6 | 7 | 8 | 9 | 10 |
|---|---|---|---|---|---|---|---|---|---|---|---|
| | Caption | | | | | | | | | | |

I'd generally suggest at the minimum setting heading 1 to level 1, heading 2 to level 2, and heading 3 to level 3. Note that this dialogue gives you a lot of control over what styles appear in the table of contents.

**Styles**

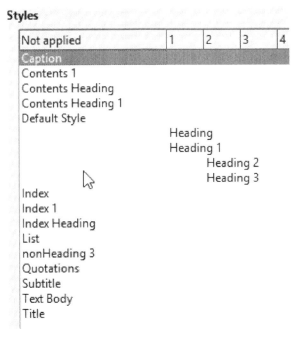

Click on OK when you're happy with the styles you are including in the table of contents.

There's an option that's interesting at the end of the index/tables tab called ☑ Index marks . While I'll descuss this later on in the chapter, an index mark is essentially a way of telling LibreOffice that there is an item that you want to include at the index at the back of the book. Leaving index marks toggled on when you're producing a table of contents can sometimes be a bad idea because you'll end up with dozens of items per chapter. Sometimes, you'll find it's better to toggle off this option. It's up to you.

Once you're happy, click OK in the insert Index/Tables dialogue.

| Table of Contents | |
|---|---|
| My first heading | 1 |
| First heading subheading 2 | 1 |
| Table of Contents | 1 |
| My Second heading | 1 |
| My Third heading | 1 |

Note that as you change the contents of your document the table of contents will become out of date, and you can update to reflect these changes by right clicking on the table and clicking on

Update Index/Table . You can change your mind about any of the above options by right clicking on the table and then clicking on

Edit Index/Table If you want to delete the table right click on

it and then click on Delete Index/Table .

### How to make an Index

An index is a list of items and page numbers often found at the end of a book or a section of a book.

In the past it used to take weeks to make an index for a complicated book. Now, LibreOffice will make and automatically update one for you in minutes.

There are two steps to making an index:

- Setting Index Entry for the text that you want to include in the document and,
- Inserting the index.

### Adding Index Entry to a document

An index entry shows LibreOffice what items you want to include in the document's index. Simply select the text you want to add an index for, e.g.  then hover over indexes and tables in the insert menu and click on entry.

You'll see the Insert Index Entry dialogue. As a rule I suggest leaving alone.

The Entry field contains the text that the index will display. By default it is the text that you highlighted. 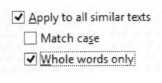 but you could change this to add extra information, e.g.

Entry    LibreOffice Impress

☑ Main entry specifies that this is the main entry for that particular index entry. If you have multiple items of the same text I'd suggest just highlighting the word once for the page that contains the most relevant item about that text, and then toggling apply to all similar texts on, and whole words only. Obviously, you'd also toggle on Match case where the case is important but that isn't often the case.

☑ Apply to all similar texts
☐ Match case
☑ Whole words only

Once you're happy click Insert .the text will change so the index entry items are highlighted:

This book is all about LibreOffice and will help you learn everything you need to know to make the program works.

LibreOffice Impress

LibreOffice Impress is a presentation tool

And when you hover your mouse over one of the highlighted words you'll see a tooltip saying that it is an index entry and the index entry name:

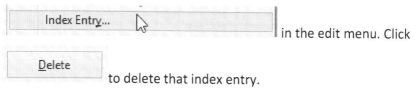

Sometimes, when you're making an index using the apply to all similar texts you might accidentally create an index entry that you don't want. Select the unwanted index entry, then click on

Index Entry...

in the edit menu. Click

Delete

to delete that index entry.

## Insert the index

First, make sure you go to the place in the document where you want to insert your index.

Hover your mouse over Indexes and tables in the insert menu, and then click on the Index and Tables to the right of the arrow ( see illustration below)

Make sure you are on the Index/Table tab in the insert index/table dialogue by clicking on it if necessary.

Click on the type box  and then select
Alphabetical Index:

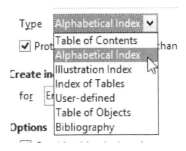

I suggest you leave Protected against manual changes toggled on. As in
inserting a table of contents you can choose to create an index for a
chapter or the entire document, but in practise I think you'd almost
always create an index for the entire document

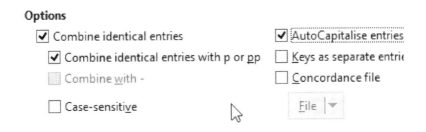

You have a lot of options. I generally suggest the following settings:

**Options**

☑ Combine identical entries            ☑ AutoCapitalise entries
   ☑ Combine identical entries with p or pp    ☐ Keys as separate entrie
   ☐ Combine with -                    ☐ Concordance file
☐ Case-sensitive                       File ▼

This will mean all items (whatever case) will be combined together with
p or pp as appropriate and that entries will be capitalised. You can vary

these settings which work pretty much as you'd expect them to.

Similarly, I don't suggest that you change the Sort options.

**Sort**

Language  English (UK)  ⌄    Key type  Alphanumeric ⌄

Click OK when you're happy with your choices. You'll see the index appear:

**Alphabetical Index**

LibreOffice............................................................................................1

LibreOffice Impress...............................................................................1

You can right click on it and select  Update Index/Table  to make the table reflect any changes you've made to the document, or

Edit Index/Table  to change any of the choices you made while inserting the index, or  Delete Index/Table  to delete the index.

## How to make a bibliography

To make a bibliography you need to insert a bibliography entry, and then insert a bibliography table.

A bibliography entry can be created in a document, or in a database that is available to all the documents you write. This user guide is only going to describe how to create a bibliography entry for a specific document since databases are outside of its scope.

## To create a bibliography entry

Go to the point in the document where you want to insert the bibliography entry. Hover over Indexes and tables in the insert menu and chose Bibliography Entry.

This will show the Insert Bibliography Entry dialogue. Make sure you

select 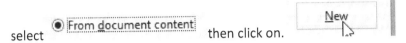 then click on. **New**

You will see the define bibliography entry dialogue. Short Name is the name of that entry. Since LibreOffice will display this when you insert it as a bibliography entry make sure you use the correct format for your name... i.e. the format you want LibreOffice to display.

Fill in the rest of the fields as appropriate, leaving any that are not applicable blank.

Press OK to add the new bibliography entry to the store in your document.

## To modify a bibliography entry

Open the Insert Bibliography Entry dialogue as above. Select the bibliography entry you want to modify from the list you get when clicking the down arrow:

Then click on **Edit** .The Define Bibliography Entry dialogue will display, edit the fields you want to change and click on OK.

## To Insert a Bibliography Entry into your document

Once you've created a Bibliography Entry it's simple to add it to the document. First, go to the place in the document where you want to add the entry. Then open the Bibliography Entry dialogue and select the short name from the list:

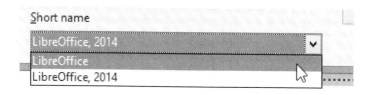

Finally then click on Insert . You'll see the bibliography entry appears in the document

### Libre Office Writer

This book is all about LibreOffice and will[LibreOffice, 2014] help you learn everything you need to know to make the program works.

## To insert the Bibliography table in the book

Hover your mouse over Index and tables in the insert menu, and then click on Indexes and tables... after the right arrow (see illustration below)

Make sure that you are on the Index/Table tab Index/Table if necessary by clicking on it.

Click on the down arrow next to the type box

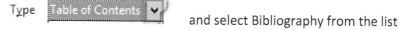 and select Bibliography from the list

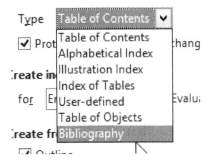

Leave all the other options at their default settings, and then press OK.

## How to insert a footnote or endnote

A footnote is a note at the end of the current page, an endnote is a note at the end of the document.

You can insert a footnote by clicking on Footnote/Endnote... in the insert menu.

This opens the Footnote/Endnote dialogue:

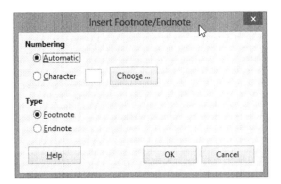

Click on the round circle by either Endnote or Footnote to choose whether to insert a footnote or endnote. This will toggle between the choices (the current choice is shown by ⊙)

Click OK.

If you are inserting a footnote, a letter you'll be taken to the bottom of the document where you will type in your footnote

When you've finished typing in the footnote press ![icon] in the icon bar (it's located to the right of the text formatting options) to return to where you were editing in the document.

LibreOffice automatically inserted a number in supertext by your footnote.

It works in the same way if you select endnote; the only difference is the text that you add will go at the end of the document and by default LibreOffice will use a letter rather than a number to denote a endnote.

### Next Chapter

In this chapter I've shown you how to generate automatically updated tables of content, indexes, and bibliographies.

The next chapter will show how to automatically generate different types of document, how to change page properties such as paper size, and how to print.

# 12 PAGE SETUP, DOCUMENT WIZARDS, AND ENVELOPES

So far in the book we've covered how to edit, save, format and illustrate documents. We've even covered how to print them. So by now you should know almost everything that you need in order to use LibreOffice effectively.

In this chapter we're going to cover a few additional features in LibreOffice that allow you to make standard documents, control what you print, and page layout.

- Set up a page (i.e. control its size, its borders and orientation)
- Choose a printer
- Print specific pages in the document
- Use the Auto document wizards to make common documents quickly

## How to Set Up a Page

In the Format menu select Page….

The first thing you'll see is the paper format options. You can either use a standard format, such as A4, or specify a particular width or height.

**Paper format**

Format:  | A4 | ⌄ |

Width:  | 21.00cm | ⬍ |

Height:  | 29.70cm | ⬍ |

There are a lot of different Formats to choose from, including envelopes and US paper sizes as well as UK paper sizes.

In general I'd suggest only using Width or Height when you are using a custom (non-standard) format.

The next option orientation. Portrait is book shaped while landscape is the traditional format for a landscape painting.

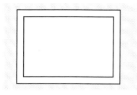

Orientation:   ⦿ Portrait
              ○ Landscape

The ⦿ denotes the current choice. If you want to choose the other one (landscape in the above example) click on the ○ .

LibreOffice puts a blank space around the text area. This is called a 'margin' and is used if you want to write notes, bind the document, or protect your document against finger marks. You can change the custom margins by editing the appropriate field in the Margins options

**Margins**

The layout settings specify whether the current layout should involve left hand pages, right hand pages, both, or mirrored pages.

Mirrored pages are where the margins are reversed in the left hand page. I.e. if on the left hand page your left hand margin is 2 and your right hand margin is 3 with a mirrored layout the right hand page will have a left hand margin of 3 and a right hand margin of 2

**NOTE:** We've shown page styles in a different part of the book. Because left hand pages and right hand pages can have different styles and different appearances selecting a Page layout of left or right will affect the appearance of your document. If you chose left hand in the page layout all your pages in the document will have a left hand page style.

When editing a page style you should be careful to make sure that you don't unintentionally override any options you've chosen in the Page Setup dialogue as otherwise your document will look pretty odd when you print it out!

## Printer Setup

I've already shown you how to print a document to the default printer. You can choose a specific printer by clicking on

 in the File menu. The Printer Setup dialogue appears. Chose your printer by clicking on the down arrow next to name.

Name ⬚ HP Deskjet 1050 J410 series ⬚ .

If you press the [Properties...] button you can chose the paper source, and what type of paper you're using. LibreOffice may change the resolution of document depending on the quality of the media. Some media's allow finer quality than others.

Clicking on the [Advanced...] button in the properties dialogue allows you to force the paper output into a specific size, force the printer to print in greyscale (shades of black or white) or black only, and also only print left or right pages.

## Advanced Printing

I've already shown you that pressing 🖶 sends the whole document to the printer. But if you want to control which printer you print to, how many (and which) pages you want to print, or the number of copies you need to use the Print Dialogue. Press ctrl+P to open it, or click

 Print...        Ctrl+P in the file menu.

Make sure you are in the General tab for the following options.

*Printer List*

To change the default printer, select the one you want in the Printer List. Note that clicking on Properties opens up the Printer Setup dialogue.

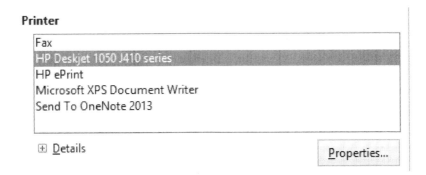

Change the number in Number of copies [1] to set how many copies of the document LibreOffice will send to the printer.

*Specifying which pages to print*

In range and copies ● All pages   means that you will print all the pages in the document.

● Pages  Allows you to decide precisely which pages you will print.

You can either use a comma separated list i.e.

● Pages  [2,3]   to specify the pages, or a range

● Pages  [2-3]   where both the first page, every page in between and the last page are printed. You can also use a combination of the two options, for example

● Pages  [2-3,1]
.

If you specify the same page twice it will print it twice.

◯ S̲election    will print only the text that you selected prior to clicking on print.

Sometimes you may want to reverse the order of the pages. You can do this by toggling ☐ Print i̲n reverse page order .

*Print more than one page per sheet*
If you want to print more than one page per sheet by scaling down the size of each page go to the | Page Layout | tab and change the number in

◉ P̲ages per s̲heet: | 1          ⌄ | . I think that it often looks better if you toggle ☐ Draw a̲ border around each page on.

*Printing to File*
When you want to print to file go to the | Options | tab, and toggle on ☐ P̲rint to file . This can be useful when you want to send a document as an attachment without necessarily allowing people to edit it.

**Use the Auto document wizards to make common documents quickly**
Sometimes you may want to make documents that are very common, such as Fax's, letters, or web pages. If you hover your mouse over wizards in the file menu you'll see a list of options to create these standard documents.

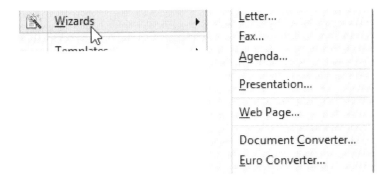

*Letters*

Hover your mouse over Wizards in the file menu, then click on letter...

**Step 1**

You'll see the Letter Wizard. The first step you choose between

( ) **Business letter** , ○ Formal personal letter and ○ Personal letter . If

your choice isn't already selected, click on the ○ to select it (the

chosen option will have ( ) beside it).

If you're writing a professional letter and your paper already has printed

letter heads toggle ☐ Use paper with pre-printed letterhead elements on

by clicking the square. You can change the look of the letter by clicking

on the arrow in Page design Elegant ▼ .

Note that you can see the letter you're making behind the dialogue.

*Note* that the next steps depend on what type of letter you've chosen.
Some steps may be bypassed for particular letter designs.

When you're happy, click next.

**Step 2**

This only applies if you toggled

☐ Use paper with pre-printed letterhead elements on in the last step. Enter the dimensions of the Logo and/or pre-printed address in this step.

You can toggle the logo off by clicking the tick ☑ Logo otherwise, enter your logo's size in the boxes provided

Height: 4.00 ⬍ Spacing to left margin: 0.00 ⬍

Width: 5.00 ⬍ Spacing to top margin: -3.40 ⬍

If you haven't pre-printed your address you can toggle it off by clicking the tick in ☑ Return address otherwise enter your addresses' size and position in the boxes provided

Height: 4.00 ⬍ Spacing to left margin: 6.00 ⬍

Width: 15.00 ⬍ Spacing to top margin: -3.40 ⬍

Toggle off ☑ Return address in envelope window if you don't want the return address included in the envelope window. In my experience it's not common to do this in the UK, and so I would toggle this field off by clicking the tick. But other people's personal preferences might vary.

If your letter has a pre-printed footer, you can adjust the height, otherwise I'd suggest toggling it off by clicking the tick. Lots of letters do have pre-printed footers with information about the company.

☑ Include footer          Height:          3.10 ⬍

Click next when you're satisfied.

**Step 3**

In Step 3 you can choose what items your letter will contain. Toggle items off (so LibreOffice doesn't include the item in the letter) by clicking a square with a tick in it, i.e. click on the highlight

 . Click on an empty square to toggle the item on (i.e. include the item).

Click next when you're happy.

**Step 4**

In the next step, click Next. NOTE: You can use this step while mail merging which I'll explain later in the chapter.

**Step 5**

This step depends on whether you're inserting a footer or not. You will skip this step if you chose to include a pre-printed footer at an earlier step.

If you're inserting a footer type into the box provided.

Footer

> This is a footer

You can toggle on or off page numbers in footers, and you can also turn off footers on the first page of the document.

**Step 6**

This step creates a template based on your previous settings. You can then edit the template manually, or simply create documents from the template. In future you won't need to go through the steps in the Letter wizard - simply create a letter from the template name.

Enter the template name

Template name:        Letter Template

Then choose if you want to create a new letter, or make changes to the template.

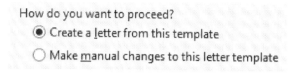

How do you want to proceed?
● Create a letter from this template
○ Make manual changes to this letter template

*Fax*

You can automatically create a fax template by hovering over wizard in the File menu, and then clicking Fax. This starts up the Fax Wizard.

**Step 1**

Chose between ● Business Fax and ○ Personal Fax by clicking on the circle.

Then select the Page Design you want by clicking on the down arrow

Page design        Classic Fax        ▼

Click next

**Step 2**

Toggle off items you don't want to include in the fax by clicking on ☑.

If you change your mind click on the square again ☐ to toggle it back on. Click next when happy.

**Step 3**

Click on the circle next to ⭕ New return address . Then enter in the return address in the appropriate boxes:

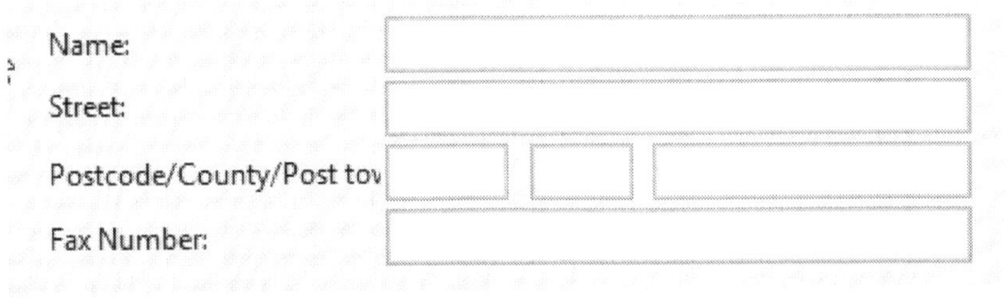

| | |
|---|---|
| Name: | |
| Street: | |
| Postcode/County/Post tov | |
| Fax Number: | |

Leave the new return address options alone - you can use these to set up a mail merge, but these options are too advanced for this book.

Click next when happy.

## Step 4

Enter a footer in the box provided.

Footer

This is a footer

You can choose to prevent it printing the footer on the first page, and whether or not to include the page number.

Click  next when happy.

## Step 5

This step makes a template from the options you've chosen. You can then either create a fax from the template or manually edit it.

First enter the template name

| Template Name: | My Fax Template |
|---|---|

Then choose between making a manual change to the fax template or creating a fax by clicking in the circle for the appropriate option.

○ Create a fax from this template

◉ Make manual changes to this fax template

Click on Finish to either make the fax or edit the template.

You can use the template you've created with this wizard in the same way as any other template.

### Other Wizards

You can also create a Agenda using the agenda wizard (Hover your mouse over Wizards in the file menu and then click on Agenda... ) and Web Page wizards. These are pretty easy to create using a similar step by step process to the Letter and Fax wizards which are more commonly used.

Selecting Presentation will open LibreOffice Impress.

## So Long, and thanks!

Well, that's it.

In this book I hope that you've learned the basics of using LibreOffice Writer. You should be able to write, edit, format and illustrate text then save or print it out.  While I haven't covered everything that LibreOffice has to offer I hope that I've covered everything you need to start using it.

I really enjoyed writing this book, and I hope that you enjoy using LibreOffice writer! If you've got any questions or comments feel free to email me at thomasecclestone@yahoo.co.uk .

# ABOUT THE AUTHOR

Thomas Ecclestone is a software programmer and technical writer from Kent in the south east of England. In his spare time he looks after a herd of Hebridean sheep and lives on a smallholding where he writes book and looks after a wildflower meadow.

You can find out more about his current projects at thomasecclestone.co.uk

40143247R00119

Made in the USA
Lexington, KY
26 March 2015